John Mac Donald

The school-room search-light

John Mac Donald

The school-room search-light

ISBN/EAN: 9783337270810

Printed in Europe, USA, Canada, Australia, Japan

Cover: Foto ©Andreas Hilbeck / pixelio.de

More available books at **www.hansebooks.com**

No. I.

The
School-
Room

SEARCH LIGHT

Test
Questions
and
Answers.

·◊·

Published by

John MacDonald,

Topeka, Kas.

County Examination Questions,

No. 1,

Contains all the questions prepared by the State Board of Education of Kansas, from the examination of August 26 and 27, 1892, to that of August 25 and 26, 1893.

County Examination Questions,

No. 2,

Contains all the question from the examination of October 28, 1893, to that of August 25, 1894.

THE ANSWERS ARE GIVEN TO ALL THE QUESTIONS,

And there are in each book seven complete sets of examinations, each set comprising 12 branches.

Price of one book, postage prepaid, 35 cents ; of both books, postage prepaid, 60 cents.

ADDRESS,

Western School Journal,

TOPEKA, KAS.

The
School=Room
Search=Light.

BETWEEN 700 AND 800 TEST QUESTIONS,
WITH ANSWERS TO ALL,

IN ARITHMETIC, LANGUAGE AND GRAMMAR, GEOGRAPHY,
UNITED STATES HISTORY, AND GENERAL
INFORMATION.

ALSO,

NINETEEN LISTS OF WORDS FOR PRONOUNCING
CONTESTS.

TOPEKA, KAS.:
JOHN MACDONALD.
1895.

ERRATUM.

In Question 3, page 126, "Rogers" should be *Young.*

NOTE.

Question No. 5, General Information, page 11, has reference to those who were in office in April, 1894.

Question No. 9, United States history, page 43, has reference to those who were in Congress in August, 1894.

In Answer No. 4, page 5, the sixth line should read:
this, with local taxation, sustains an excellent system

PRESS OF THE KANSAS STATE PRINTING COMPANY,
TOPEKA, KAS.

PREFACE.

IN this book are collected all the Test Questions and Answers which appeared in the WESTERN SCHOOL JOURNAL during the 19 months ending August, 1895. These questions—numbering more than 700—are in arithmetic, language and grammar, geography, United States history, and general information. The purpose in preparing them was to furnish teachers a large variety of questions suitable for reviewing classes, or for miscellaneous exercises on Friday afternoons, or for opening exercises in the mornings.

Besides 19 sets of questions, the book contains 19 lists of words commonly mispronounced. These are intended to be used at pronouncing contests. If the regulations on page 9 are followed, the contests can be made entertaining and valuable.   JOHN MACDONALD.

TOPEKA, KAS., September, 1895.

INDEX.

	PAGE.		PAGE.
No. 1.—Questions	1	No. 10.—Answers	81
Answers	4	No. 11.—Questions	86
No. 2.—Questions	10	Answers	89
Answers	12	No. 12.—Questions	94
No. 3.—Questions	16	Answers	96
Answers	19	No. 13.—Questions	101
No. 4.—Questions	24	Answers	104
Answers	27	No. 14.—Questions	111
No. 5.—Questions	33	Answers	114
Answers	36	No. 15.—Questions	119
No. 6.—Questions	42	Answers	122
Answers	45	No. 16.—Questions	128
No. 7.—Questions	54	Answers	131
Answers	56	No. 17.—Questions	137
No. 8.—Questions	62	Answers	140
Answers	64	No. 18.—Questions	145
No. 9.—Questions	71	Answers	147
Answers	73	No. 19.—Questions	152
No. 10.—Questions	79	Answers	155

PRONOUNCING CONTEST......... 8, 15, 23, 32, 41, 53, 61, 70, 78, 85
93, 100, 110, 118, 127, 136, 144, 151, 158

REGULATIONS GOVERNING PRONOUNCING CONTESTS............... 9

ARITHMETIC:
Questions.................. 1, 10, 16, 24, 33, 42, 54, 62, 71, 79
86, 94, 101, 111, 119, 128, 137, 145, 152

Answers................... 4, 12, 19, 27, 36, 45, 56, 64, 73, 81
89, 96, 104, 114, 122, 131, 140, 147, 155

LANGUAGE AND GRAMMAR:
Questions.................. 1, 10, 16, 24, 33, 42, 54, 62, 71, 79
86, 94, 102, 112, 119, 128, 137, 145, 152

Answers................... 4, 12, 20, 28, 36, 46, 57, 66, 74, 81
90, 97, 105, 114, 122, 131, 140, 148, 155

GEOGRAPHY:
Questions.................. 2, 11, 17, 25, 34, 43, 55, 63, 72, 79
87, 95, 102, 112, 120, 129, 138, 146, 153

Answers................... 5, 13, 21, 29, 37, 47, 59, 66, 74, 82
91, 97, 106, 115, 124, 133, 141, 149, 156

UNITED STATES HISTORY:
Questions.................. 3, 11, 17, 25, 34, 43, 55, 63, 72, 80
88, 95, 103, 113, 120, 129, 139, 146, 153

Answers................... 6, 13, 21, 30, 38, 47, 59, 67, 75, 82
92, 98, 107, 116, 124, 134, 142, 149, 157

GENERAL INFORMATION:
Questions.................. 3, 11, 18, 26, 35, 44, 56, 64, 73, 80
88, 95, 103, 113, 121, 130, 139, 147, 154

Answers................... 7, 14, 21, 30, 39, 50, 60, 68, 76, 83
92, 99, 108, 116, 125, 135, 143, 150, 157

Arithmetic —(1) How many slates will be required to cover a roof, each side of which is 34 feet 9 inches long and 16 feet wide, allowing 4 slates to cover a square foot; and what will they cost at the rate of $4.75 per hundred?

(2) A teacher, in grading the examination papers of a class of five, marked as follows: 57, 35, 68, 75, 27. The pupil who made no mistake was to receive 85 marks. What percentage of the questions did each answer?

(3) Two trains, one 210 feet long, and the other 230, move on parallel tracks. When going in the same direction, they pass each other in 15 seconds; and when going in opposite directions, they pass in 3¾ seconds. Find the rates of the trains.—*Elwood's Table Book and Test Problems.*

Language and Grammar.—(1) Give the feminine of tyrant, victor, instructor.

(2) Give three nouns that have the same termination for masculine and feminine, and three that are used only in the feminine.

(3) From what languages are the following words derived: Crag, mortgage, philosophy, convene, absolve, avalanche, courier?

(4) Write a composition of not less than 500 words on your favorite poet, telling why you prefer him or her to other poets.

(5) Punctuate correctly the following: Thou art an honest fellow replied the robber I warrant thee and we worship not St. Nicholas so devoutly but what thy thirty zechins may yet escape if thou deal uprightly with us meantime render up thy trust for the time so saying he took from Gurth's breast the large leathern pouch in which the purse given him by Rebecca was inclosed as well as the rest of the zechins and then continued his interrogation who is thy master.— *Ivanhoe.*

Geography.—(1) Describe in a composition not exceeding 500 words Rio Janeiro and harbor. Let a map accompany the composition.

(2) What is the form of goverment in San Domingo? The prevailing religion?

(3) What is the form of government in Tibet, Sumatra, Persia, Borneo, Egypt?

(4) What provision has been made for the education of children in Switzerland, Argentine Republic, Spain, Sweden, Turkey?

(5) What is meant by the terms "spring tides" and "neap tides?"

United States History.—(1) Name the governments which have had possession of New Orleans, and tell how long a period it was held by each.

(2) When was the patent office established? Before that time, by what department were patents issued?

(3) Name the ships that gave rise to the Alabama claims, and name the arbitrators who arbitrated the claims at Geneva.

(4) Name one secretary of war and five secretaries of state, each of whom afterward became President of the United States.

(5) Has an income tax ever been levied in the United States? If so, when was it levied, and what were its main features?

(6) Explain these terms in United States history: Loco-foco, ku-klux klan, know-nothing party, barnburners.

General Information.—(1) For how long a period is an author granted copyright in the United States?

(2) Name all the world's expositions, and tell where each was held.

(3) What is meant by extradition? Give an illustration.

(4) What do the words "bastille," "barricades" and "lettres de cachet" suggest to you?

(5) What is the difference between common and statute law?

ANSWERS TO TEST QUESTIONS
No. 1.

Arithmetic.—(1) $34.75 \times 16 \times 4 = 2224$. $\$4.75 \times 22.24 = \$105.64$.

(2) $67+$; $41+$; $80+$; $88+$; $31+$.

(3) Let A denote the faster train, B the other. Then, to pass B when going the same way, A must gain $230 + 210 = 440$ feet, and $440 \div 15 = 29\frac{1}{3}$ feet, which is A's excess of rate per second. In opposite directions, they together move 440 feet in $3\frac{3}{4}$ seconds, or $117\frac{1}{3}$ feet per second, of which A runs $29\frac{1}{3}$ feet more than B. Then $\frac{1}{2}$ of $(117\frac{1}{3} - 29\frac{1}{3}) = 44 =$ B's rate per second, and $44 + 29\frac{1}{3} = 73\frac{1}{3}$, A's rate. $(44 \times 3600) \div 5280 = 30$ (miles per hour), and $(73\frac{1}{3} \times 3600) \div 5280 = 50$ (miles per hour), the required rates.

Language and Grammar.—(1) Tyraness, victress, instructress.

(2) Parent, witness, friend. (*a*) Brunette, milliner, Amazon.

(3) Celtic, French, Greek, Latin, Latin, French, French.

(5) "Thou art an honest fellow," replied the robber, "I warrant thee; and we worship not St. Nicholas so devoutly ｜ · what thy thirty zechins may yet escape, if thou deal uprightly with us. Meantime render up thy trust for the time." So saying, he

took from Gurth's breast the large leather. pouch, in which the purse given him by Rebecca was inclosed, as well as the rest of the zechins, and then continued his interrogation, "Who is thy master?"

Geography.—(2) (a) Republican. (b) Catholic.

(3) (a) It is a dependency of China; hence has a despotic form. (b) It is a dependency of Holland. (c) Despotic. (d) It is a dependency of Holland, and Holland has a limited monarchy, though probably the government in both Sumatra and Borneo is despotic. (e) It is tributary to Turkey, but is virtually independent. The government is despotic.

(4) (a) The constitution of Switzerland requires education to be sufficient, obligatory, gratuitous, unsectarian, and under public control of the state. Funds are provided by the state and the commune. (b) The national congress makes an appropriation; with local taxation, sustains an xllent systemhis,e the of schools. (c) Education is compulsory and free, but the law is not well enforced. Teachers are poorly paid. (d) Education is compulsory and free. The law provides for a school in every parish. The results are excellent. (e) The government has done little or nothing.

(5) At new moon and at full moon the sun and moon exert their power on the tides in the same direction; hence the tides are highest and lowest. These are known as "spring tides." At the quarters

of the moon, the sun and moon are exerting power in opposite directions; hence the tides do not rise as high nor sink so low. These are known as "neap tides."

United States History.—(1) France, from 1718 to 1768; Spain, from 1768 to November, 1803; France, again, about 20 days.

(2) (*a*) 1836. (*b*) Until 1793 by the secretary of war, the secretary of state, and the attorney general; from 1793 to 1836 by the secretary of state; after 1836 by the commissioner of patents.

(3) (*a*) Sumter, Florida, Alabama, Georgia, Shenandoah. (*b*) Count Frederigo Sclopis, Italy; Baron Itajubo, Brazil; Jacques Staempfli, Switzerland; Charles Francis Adams, United States; Sir Alexander Cockburn, Great Britain.

(4) (*a*) James Monroe. (*b*) Thomas Jefferson, James Madison, James Monroe, John Quincy Adams, Martin Van Buren.

(5) On August 5, 1861, an act of Congress authorized a tax of 3 per cent. on all incomes over $800 a year. In July, 1862, the law was amended, and all incomes under $5,000 were taxed 5 per cent., with an exemption of $600 and house rent. Incomes from $5,000 to $10,000 were taxed 2½ per cent. additional —that is, 7½ per cent.— with no exemptions; incomes above $10,000 were taxed 5 per cent. additional, with no exemption. Various amendments were made after the war. The tax expired in 1872.

(6) (*a*) The radical wing of the democratic party, in 1835-'37. The term originated in New York, and was derived from a particular kind of matches. Subsequently the name was given to the national democratic party. (*b*) A secret, oath-bound organization formed in the South in 1866 or 1867. Its object was to prevent negroes from voting or holding office. (*c*) A secret, oath-bound association, known also as the American party. It was formed in 1852, and lasted until about the beginning of the war. The main object of the party was to prevent foreign-born citizens from holding office. Finally merged into the freesoil party. (*d*) The barnburners were radical in views, and were so named from a story of a farmer who burned his barn to get rid of the rats.

General Information. — (1) 28 years, with the privilege of renewal for 14 years.

(2) The first exposition was held in London, in 1851; the second in Paris, in 1855; the third in London, in 1862; the fourth in Paris, in 1867; the fifth in Vienna, in 1873; the sixth in Philadelphia, in 1876; the seventh in Paris, in 1878; the eighth in New Orleans, in 1884-'85; the ninth in Chicago, in 1893.

(4) The delivering up to justice of fugitive criminals by the authorities of one country to those of another. If a criminal should flee from France to the United States, he would be delivered to the French government, on the request being made and proofs

presented. (*a*) A French prison at Paris which had become odious to the people, because it was into its dungeons the French tyrants cast their victims. It was destroyed early in the French revolution. (*b*) A French term applied to obstructions placed across streets for defensive purposes. (*c*) Letters or papers, signed by the French monarch, authorizing the arbitrary imprisonment of the person named. *Lettres de cachet* were abolished by the assembly in 1790.

(5) Common law "is an unwritten law which receives its binding force from immemorial usage and universal reception, in distinction from the written or statute law. Its rules or principles are to be found only in the works of institutional writers, in the records of courts, and in the reports of judicial decisions, and it is overruled by the statute law."—*Cyclopedia of Political Science.*

PRONOUNCING CONTEST — No. 1.

Ultima Thule, baptism, Youghiogheny, visor, vivacious, vicar, Reykjavik, minutiæ, contumacy, contumely, aunt, ay or aye (meaning *yes*), aye (meaning *always*), soot, dysentery, placable, placard, requiem. Richelieu, sauce, sewer (one who sews), sewer (an underground drain), servile, schismatic, domicile, architrave, revocable, extempore, maligner, incomparable, indissoluble, dishabille, diastole, dilettante, consummate (adjective), consummate (verb), consignee, conspiracy, basilisk, bequeath.

Regulations Governing Pronouncing Contests.

Let sides be chosen as in spelling. Let the teacher stand behind the contestants, where it will be impossible to get suggestions from his marking. Let every pupil on each side pronounce every word in the list. Let every error in accent and sounds of letters be marked. Let the number of errors made by each side be placed on the blackboard. A new list should not be given until every contestant can pronounce every word in the old list.

TEST QUESTIONS—No. 2.

Arithmetic.—(1) How many days from January 30, 1892, to July 4, both included?

(2) What per cent. is $\frac{2}{7}$ of $\frac{9}{14}$?

(3) I buy one-fifth of an acre of land for $2,178. For how much a square foot must I sell it in order to gain 20 per cent. of the cost?—*Harvard Examination Papers.*

Language and Grammar.— 1) Give the degrees of comparison of "far" and "forth," and the difference in meaning between "farther" and "further."

(2) Give three examples of defective comparisons in adjectives.

(3) Correct the following errors, and give reasons: "If I was wealthy I should travel." "Rhode Island is not as large as Butler county, Kansas." "If the snow should be so difficult to walk through to-morrow as it is to-day, you cannot go to school."

(4) Punctuate correctly the following: Who is that said the Doctor Oh Come in Toots come in Mr. Dombey sir Toots bowed quite a coincidence said Doctor Blimber here we have the beginning and the end Alpha and Omega our head boy Mr Dombey

Geography. — (1) The Nile receives one-third more rain than the Mississippi, but the Mississippi discharges five times as much water as the Nile. Give the reason.

(2) Why have the Mediterranean and the Baltic scarcely any tides?

(3) Why is the interior of Australia a desert?

(4) What are the relations between Norway and Sweden?

United States History. — (1) How many proclamations of amnesty have been issued in the United States?

(2) How many persons named Adams are celebrated in American history? Tell something concerning each.

(3) What is meant by "repudiation" in our history? Give instances.

General Information. — (1) By what name is the national legislature known in Spain, Switzerland, Austria, Germany?

(2) To what extent is the right to vote granted in Spain, Italy, and France?

(3) What powers has the United States court of appeals?

(4) What is meant by "eminent domain"?

(5) Name the chief justice and associate justices of the supreme court of the United States.

ANSWERS TO TEST QUESTIONS
No. 2.

Arithmetic.—(1) 157.

(2) $44\frac{4}{9}\%$.

(3) 1 A. $=43,560$ sq. ft. $\frac{1}{5}$ of 43,560 sq. ft. $=8,$-712 sq. ft.   Cost of land per sq. ft. $=\$2,178 \div 8,712$ $=25$ cents.   25 cents $+ 20\% = 30$ cents.   Proof: 8,712 sq. ft. at 30 cents $=\$2,613.60$; $\$2,178 + 20\%$ $=\$2,613.60$.

___

Language and Grammar.—(1) Far, farther, farthest, farthermost; forth, further, furthest. *Farther* means more distant; *further* also means more distant, but in addition means the remoter of two things, as "the further side." It also means wider or fuller, as "further, he said."

(2) Nether, nethermost (no positive); rear (positive), rearmost (superlative), no comparative; out, outer, utter, outermost, utmost.

(3) (*a*) "If I were wealthy I would travel." *Were* is the form used for the subjunctive; *would* is used instead of *should* because a resolution is expressed. (*b*) "Rhode Island is not so large as Butler county, Kansas." *So*, with a negative, should be followed by *as*. (*c*) "If the snow should be so difficult to walk through to-morrow as it is to-day, I could not go to school." The tense of a verb in a subordinate

clause must agree with the tense of the verb in the principal clause.

(4) "Who is that?" said the doctor. "Oh! come in, Toots; come in. Mr. Dombey, sir." Toots bowed. "Quite a coincidence!" said Doctor Blimber. "Here we have the beginning and the end. Alpha and Omega. Our head boy, Mr. Dombey."

Geography.—(1) Because the Nile loses much of its water by evaporation in crossing the desert.

(2) Because the narrowness of their mouths prevents them from being much affected by the tides of the ocean.

(3) Because rain-bearing clouds cannot reach it from the ocean at the season of the year when condensation easily takes place.

(4) They have one king, but separate legislatures.

United States History.—(1) On December 8, 1863, President Lincoln issued a proclamation of amnesty. A supplementary proclamation, explanatory of the first, was issued on March 26, 1864. On May 29, 1865, President Johnson issued a proclamation offering amnesty; on September 7, 1867, another; on July 4, 1868, a third, and on December 25, 1868, a fourth. These five proclamations were to the people of the states which had been in rebellion.

(2) Samuel Adams, one of the founders of American independence. John Adams, another of the

founders of the republic; he was minister to France
and England, vice president and President of the
United States. John Quincy Adams, sixth President of the United States. Charles Francis Adams,
minister to Great Britain, 1861–'68.

(3) Refusal to pay debts incurred by states, counties, or municipalities. The word began to be used
about 55 years ago. Georgia, by constitutional amendment, prohibited the payment of debts created during
the reconstruction period. Mississippi also repudi-
ated bonds issued before the war.

———

General Information.—(1) (*a*) Cortes. (*b*) Federal assembly. (*c*) Reichsrath. (*d*) Bundensrath
and reichstag.

(2) (*a*) Every citizen 25 years of age and over
has a vote. (*b*) Must be a citizen, 25 years of age,
and be able to read and write. (*c*) Must be a citizen, and 21 years of age.

(3) The United States circuit court of appeals is a
court of appeals put in between the United States
supreme court and the United States circuit court.
The court was established to relieve the supreme
court. Its decisions are final in certain cases.

(4) Original ownership retained by the sovereign,
or remaining in the state, whereby land or other private property can be taken for the public benefit.—
Lalor's Cyclopedia of Political Science.

(5) M. W. Fuller, 1888, Ill., Cleveland, Dem.

S. J. Field, 1863, Cal., Lincoln, Dem.

J. M. Harlan, 1877, Ky., Hayes, Rep.

Horace Gray, 1881, Mass., Arthur, Rep.

D. J. Brewer, 1889, Kas., Harrison, Rep.

H. B. Brown, 1890, Mich., Harrison, Rep.

George Shiras, jr., 1892, Pa., Harrison, Rep.

H. E. Jackson, 1893, Tenn., Harrison, Dem.

E. D. White, 1894, La., Cleveland, Dem.

PRONOUNCING CONTEST—No. 2.

Viva voce, *vis-a-vis*, renaissance, unlearned (adjective), *table d'hote*, tableau, surveillance, solstice, seismic, ribald, recluse, *recherché*, premise (noun), premise (verb), plagiarism, jocose, interpolate, internecine, imbroglio, docile.

TEST QUESTIONS — No. 3.

Arithmetic.—(1) A merchant's private key for marking goods is "prevention." How must he mark goods which cost 25 cents a yard? How must he mark the selling price at 25 per cent. gain on the cost price?

(2) What is meant by the "par of exchange?"

(3) I borrow $500 at a bank for 90 days; discount 6 per cent. For what sum must I give my note to obtain the amount?

(4) A granary 24 feet long, 8 feet high and 12 feet wide lacks 40 per cent. of being full of wheat. How many more bushels of wheat will it hold?

(5) How far will a boy walk in plowing 1½ acres if his plow turns a furrow one foot wide?

Language and Grammar.—(1) Give five nouns, each of which has two plurals.

(2) Give three nouns which have in the plural one form and two meanings.

(3) Correct the following errors, and give a reason for each correction: "This is one of the mildest springs that has ever been known." "You must not act like he does." "He fell off of the barn." "Most

everybody has a cold." "Kansas City has the largest population of any other city in Kansas."

(4) What is the difference in meaning between "This is a picture of John," and "This is a picture of John's"?

(5) Define *aphorism* and *epigram*, and give an illustration of each.

Geography.—(1) Why were the trade winds so named?

(2) In what countries are the following words used: Fiord, loch, pampas, steppes? Define each word.

(3) Give the swiftness, width, temperature and color of the Gulf Stream.

(4) In what country do the people uncover the feet, instead of the head, as a mark of respect?

(5) Where is the largest tree in the world?

(6) On a voyage from New York to Hamburg, over what waters would you sail, and what countries would you pass?

United States History.—(1) What is meant by "Tammany Hall" in American politics?

(2) Name the first state admitted into the union after the first 13. Name the last state admitted.

(3) A noted author was secretary of the navy; minister to Great Britain; minister to Prussia; min-

ister to the German empire. Name him, and his
chief literary work.

(4) How many members of the United States
senate were there in 1800? How many are there
now?

(5) North Carolina did not ratify the constitution
of the United States until November 21, 1789;
Rhode Island, not until May 29, 1790. Why did
these two states delay ratification so long?

General Information.—(1) For what is each of
the following-named islands noted: Elba, Caprera,
Island No. 10?

(2) Name the author of "Comus," "Obiter
Dicta," "The Sublime and Beautiful," "John Gil-
pin," "Imaginary Conversations," "Pride and Prej-
udice."

(3) Name a poet who committed suicide by poison-
ing himself; a noted scientific investigator and writer
who shot himself; and a noted woman—eminent in
literature—who was drowned.

(4) Who painted "The Last Supper," "The
Rake's Progress," "1807," "Ecce Homo"?

(5) In what books do the following names represent characters; Dominie Sampson; John Rokesmith;
Christiana; Ichabod Crane; Becky Sharp.

(6) In which play of Shakespeare is Caliban; Au-
tolycus; Benvolio; Olivia; Christopher Sly?

(7) What can you tell concerning the following-named places: The Bridge of Sighs; Stonehenge; the Coliseum; the Alhambra; the Golden Horn?

(8) Where do we find the first mention of circuit courts?

(9) Give the meaning of each of the following expressions: *Amende honorable; au fait; hors de combat; Ultima Thule; recherché.*

(10) Who wrote: "Where ignorance is bliss 't is folly to be wise;" "Variety is the very spice of life;" "There is, however, a limit at which forbearance ceases to be a virtue."

ANSWERS TO TEST QUESTIONS
No. 3.

Arithmetic.—(1) Pe; ep $\frac{e}{v}$.

(2) The value of the currency of any country expressed in the currency of another.

(3) The proceeds of $1 for $90 + 3$ days, at 6%, are $0.9845. $500 \div .9845 = $507.87+$.

(4) $24 \times 8 \times 12 = 2,304$ cu. ft. $= 1,851$ bu. It will hold 740 bu.

(5) 1 A. $= 43,560$ sq. ft. $1\frac{1}{2}$ A. $= 65,340$ sq. ft. For every mile he walks he plows 5,280 sq. ft.; hence, 65,340 sq. ft. $\div 5,280 =$ the number of miles he travels, or about $12\frac{1}{3}$ miles.

Language and Grammar.—(1) Pennies (separate coins), pence (sum of money); indexes (tables of contents), indices (terms used in algebra); shots (discharges), shot (balls); geniuses (persons of genius), genii (spirits); brothers (by birth), brethren (of a community).

(2) Customs: (*a*) Habits; (*b*) revenue duties. Numbers: (*a*) In arithmetic; (*b*) in poetry. Pains: (*a*) Sufferings; (*b*) care.

(3) (*a*) This is one of the mildest springs that *have* ever been known. The verb must agree with its subject. (*b*) You must not act *as* he does. *Like* is not a conjunction, and is improperly used for the conjunctive adverb *as*. (*c*) He fell off the barn. *Of* is superfluous. (*d*) *Nearly* everybody has a cold. *Most* is an adjective, and is improperly used. (*e*) Kansas City has a larger population than any other city in Kansas. The superlative *largest* and the preposition *of* are wrongly used.

(4) "This is a picture of John" means "This is a likeness of John." "This is a picture of John's" means "This picture belongs to John."

(5) An aphorism is a comprehensive maxim or principle expressed in a few words, as "Smooth runs the water when the brook is deep." An epigram is a bright thought tersely and sharply expressed, whether in verse or prose.—*International Dictionary.* Illustration: "Solitude is sometimes best society."

Geography.—(1) The name was given because they blew steadily in one direction; hence, could be depended on by ships engaged in commerce.

(2) Norway; Scotland; South America, chiefly in the Argentine Republic; southeastern Europe, and in Asia.

(3) Four miles an hour; about 30 miles wide; above 80° Fahr.; deep blue.

(5) The largest tree known is a chestnut tree near the base of Mount Etna. It is 190 feet in circumference.

United States History.—(1) Tammany hall is the name of the building on Fourteenth street, New York, in which the democrats have their headquarters. In politics, the name has come to mean the democratic organization in the city of New York.

(2) (*a*) Vermont. (*b*) Wyoming.

(3) (*a*) George Bancroft. (*b*) History of the United States.

(4) (*a*) 32. (*b*) 88.

(5) North Carolina wanted a] bill of rights and amendments, and Rhode Island feared the federal constitution would destroy the state paper currency.

General Information.—(1) (*a*) The island to which Napoleon was exiled after his abdication in 1814. (*b*) The home of Garibaldi during the last part of his life. (c) It was fortified by the Confederates in the early part of the civil war. It was situated a few miles below Columbus, Ky., and commanded the river. The island was captured by General Pope and Commodore Foote on April 7, 1862.

(2) John Milton; Augustus Birrell; Edmund Burke; William Cowper; Walter Savage Landor; Jane Austen.

(3) Thomas Chatterton; Hugh Miller; Margaret Fuller Ossoli.

(4) Leonardo da Vinci; William Hogarth; Jean Louis Ernest Meissonier; Antonio Allegri da Correggio.

(5) "Guy Mannering;" "Our Mutual Friend;" "The Pilgrim's Progress;" "Sketch Book;" "Vanity Fair."

(6) "The Tempest;" "Winter's Tale;" "Romeo and Juliet;" "Twelfth Night;" "Taming of the Shrew."

(7) (a) It connects the palace of the doge with the state prisons of Venice, and is so called because state prisoners were conveyed over it from the judgment hall to the place of execution. (b) The remnants of two circles of huge stones on Salisbury Plain, Wiltshire, England. Stonehenge is supposed to have been a Druidical temple. (c) An amphitheater in Rome, erected by Nero. Its ruins are probably the finest in the world. (d) A palace of the Moorish kings of Granada. For a description of the ruins, see the

writings of Washington Irving. (e) The curve in the Bosphorus, on which Constantinople is situated.

(8) I Samuel, vii, 16: "And he went from year to year in circuit to Bethel and Gilgal and Mizpah, and judged Israel in all those places."

(9) (a) A satisfactory apology. (b) Up to the mark. (c) Out of condition to fight. (d) The utmost boundary or limit. (e) Choice; of rare elegance.

(10) (a) Thomas Gray. (b) William Cowper. (c) Edmund Burke.

PRONOUNCING CONTEST—No. 3.

Obligatory, *bona fide*, divan, grimaces, Messonier, Disraeli, commandant, objurgato, nepotism, morphine, research, dynamite, wiseacre, viscount, vehement, subtile, subtle, scenic, glacial, glacier.

TEST QUESTIONS—No. 4.

Arithmetic.—(1) I owe Mr. A. in New York $50. I go to a bank in Topeka, pay $50, and receive a draft on a New York bank. This draft I send to Mr. A. Why does the New York bank pay the draft? What must Mr. A. do before receiving the cash?

(2) When it is 9 A. M. in Boston, what is the time at San Francisco?

(3) A merchant's private key for marking goods is "promulgate." If he buy goods at $12\frac{1}{2}$ cents a yard, how should the cost price be marked? How must he mark the selling price if he sells at a gain of 10 per cent.?

(4) A grocer buys syrup at 80 cents a gallon, and sells it at 12 cents a pint. How much per cent. does he gain?

(5) A farmer bought the south half of the southwest quarter of the southwest quarter of section 20, town 12, range 15, at $18 an acre. He sold the tract for $450. What was his per cent. of gain or loss? Make a diagram.

Language and Grammar.—(1) Illustrate the difference between the use of the word "observation" and "observance."

(2) Why is it wrong to use the following words: *Illy, enthuse,* Sundayed.

(3) Define *idiom,* and give three idiomatic expressions.

(4) Correct these expressions, and give a reason for each correction: "Either of the three;" "I expect you were surprised I did not come yesterday;" "He is very pleased with his teacher;" "The Pickwick Papers were written by Chas. Dickens;" "They act like they were angry."

(5) Give an example of *simile, metaphor, personification.*

———

Geography.—(1) State briefly the difference between a cyclone and a tornado.

(2) What are land-and-sea breezes? What causes them?

(3) Name in the order of value the five chief exports of the United States.

(4) Compare Japan and China as to characteristics of the people, language, and religion.

(5) A certain territory, having an independent government, has an area of but 8.34 square miles. Name it, give its boundaries, and tell for what it is noted.

———

United States History.—(1) A certain American, of foreign birth, was instructor in Harvard College; secretary of the treasury; minister from the United

States to France; minister from the United States to Great Britain. Name him, his native land, and any important public service he may have done.

(2) Name all the Presidents of the United States who were soldiers.

(3) Name the states which seceded from the union, and arrange the list so as to show the order in which they seceded.

(4) A certain vice president of the United States had his name changed by legislative enactment when he was 18 years of age. Name him.

(5) A noted advocate of state sovereignty was successively representative in congress; secretary of war; vice president; United States senator; secretary of state; United States senator (a second time). Name him.

———

General Information.—(1) In what books do the following names represent characters: Hester Prynn, Rowena, Dinah Morris, Jack Bunsby, Emilé?

(2) In history, what is meant by each of the following terms: "The Hundred Days;" "The Monroe Doctrine;" "The Sick Man of the East;" "The Balance of Power;" "Consequential Damages"?

(3) In which play of Shakespeare is Moth; Cordelia; Dogberry; Parolles; Benedick?

(4) Substitute the right name for each of the following: "The Great Unknown;" "The Great

Cham of Literature;" "Charles Egbert Craddock;" "Elia;" "Uncle Remus."

(5) Name a noted poet who was drowned, and whose body, when washed ashore, was cremated.

(6) Name the author of "Wuthering Heights;" "Levana;" "Sohrab and Rustum;" "The Princess;" "Rise of the Dutch Republic."

(7) For what were the following-named persons noted: Murillo, Comenius, Mozart, Audubon, Tasso?

(8) What are the "fine arts"?

(9) What is meant by "balance of trade"?

(10) What is meant by "pirate" in literature?

ANSWERS TO TEST QUESTIONS
No. 4.

Arithmetic.—(1) (a) Because the Topeka bank has in the New York bank a deposit wherewith to meet drafts. (b) He must indorse the draft, and in some cases must be identified.

(2) Longitude of San Francisco, 122° 26′ 15″; of Boston, 71° 3′ 30″; both west longitude. The difference in longitude = 51° 22′ 45″. 51° 22′ 45″ ÷ 15 = 3 hr. 25 min. 31 sec. (For another method, see p. 131, May number WESTERN SCHOOL JOURNAL.)

(3) Pr $\frac{p}{r}$; po $\frac{o}{m}$.

(4) 1 gallon $= 8$ pints.   12 cents $\times 8 = 96$ cents. Gain, 20 %.

(5) S. $\frac{1}{2}$ of the S. W. $\frac{1}{4}$ of the S. W. $\frac{1}{4} = 20$ acres. $18 \times 20 = \$360$. $450 - \$360 = \$90 = 25$ % gain. The pupils should make the diagram.

Language and Grammar —(1) "Observation" is the act of noticing; "observance," a celebration, as the observance of the Sabbath.

(2) Because "illy" is not sanctioned by good authority; "enthuse" is slang; and "Sundayed" exists only in the vocabulary of crude reporters.

(3) A use of words peculiar to a particular language, especially if it be an irregularity; a form of speech characteristic of a writer or a tongue.—*Standard Dictionary.* Examples: "I can *make nothing* of it." "He *treats* his subject *home.*" "It is that within us that *makes* for righteousness."

(4) (*a*) "*Any one* of the three." *Either* is used only when speaking of two objects. (*b*) "I *suppose* or *presume* you were surprised I did not come yesterday." *Expect* should be used only when one speaks of what is to come. (*c*) The adverb *very* should not be used before a passive participle. (*d*) "The Pickwick Papers" is the title of a book, hence is in the singular number, and the verb must agree with its nominative. (*e*) *Like* should not be used as a conjunction instead of *as* or *as if.*

(5) "Like as a father pitieth his children." "The hand of time falls heavily upon the red stone." "The flowers nod gaily to each other."

Geography.—(1) A cyclone is a rotatory storm, and is caused by the overheating of the air next the surface of the earth. This after a while causes an up draft, towards which the wind blows from all directions. The up draft is the center of the cyclone, or "storm center," towards which the wind blows in a spiral or whirl. The path of the cyclone is usually 3,000 miles in length; its breadth several hundred miles. A tornado is a rotatory storm which is prevalent mainly in great plains. The path of the tornado rarely exceeds 40 or 50 miles in length, and the destructive part of the whirl may be only a few rods in diameter.—*Tilden's Commercial Geography.*

(2) During the day the earth becomes heated, and reaches a higher temperature than the water. The air rises, and the air over the sea, being more condensed, blows as a sea breeze toward the land. After sunset, the land is more rapidly cooled than the water; hence the breeze blows from the land toward the sea; in other words, the condensed air flows toward the rarefied air.

(3) Cotton, flour, wheat, tobacco, corn.

(4) To be answered by the pupils in the form of essays.

(5) Monaco. It is situated on the Mediterranean,

nine miles east of Nice, and is bounded on the landward side by French territory. It is noted — or, rather, notorious — from the fact that at Monte Carlo, its chief town, there are gambling tables on a large scale, and that the little principality is sustained by the proceeds.

United States History.—(1) Albert Gallatin. He was a native of Switzerland. He negotiated the treaty of Ghent, in 1814.

(2) Washington, Monroe, Jackson, William Henry Harrison, Taylor, Grant, Hayes, Garfield, Benjamin Harrison.

(3) South Carolina, Mississippi, Florida, Alabama, Georgia, Louisiana, Texas, Arkansas, North Carolina, Virginia, Tennessee.

(4) Henry Wilson.

(5) John C. Calhoun.

General Information.—(1) "The Scarlet Letter;" "Ivanhoe;" "Adam Bede;" "Dombey and Son;" Rousseau's "Émile."

(2) (*a*) The days between Napoleon's departure from Elba, on March 20, 1815, and the day on which he abdicated, June 22, 1815. (*b*) The annual message of President Monroe, in 1823, contained the following: "With the existing colonies or dependencies of any European power we have not interfered, and

shall not interfere; but with the governments which have declared their independence and maintained it, and whose independence we have, on great consideration and just principles, acknowledged, we could not view an interposition for oppressing them, or controlling in any other manner their destiny by any European power, in any other light than as a manifestation of an unfriendly disposition toward the United States." (c) A term applied by European diplomatists to Turkey. (d) A term used in Europe. It means that no nation shall be allowed to increase its territory so as to endanger the independence of any other country. (e) Chas. Sumner, in discussing the depredations of the Alabama and other ships, asserted that England was liable for consequential or indirect damages, as well as for those directly committed. Thus, the interruption of commerce and the cost of pursuing the Confederate cruisers would be classed as consequential damages.

(3) "Love's Labor's Lost;" "King Lear;" "Much Ado About Nothing;" "All's Well that Ends Well;" "Much Ado About Nothing."

(4) Sir Walter Scott; Dr. Samuel Johnson; Mary N. Murfree; Charles Lamb; Joel Chandler Harris.

(5) Percy Bysshe Shelley.

(6) Charlotte Brontë; Jean Paul Friedrich Richter; Matthew Arnold; Alfred Tennyson; John Lothrop Motley.

(7) (a) A great artist. (b) Noted for reforms in

methods of teaching.   (c) A celebrated composer of music.   (d) A noted naturalist.   (e) A great poet.

(8) Music, painting, poetry, and sculpture.

(9) The difference in value between the exports and imports of a nation.

(10) One who publishes books or any other writings without the permission of the author.

PRONOUNCING CONTEST—No. 4.

Flagitious, acquiesce, inveighed (railed), elision, synchronous, mysticism, cataclysm, solstitial, cicerone, innoxious, emollient, tessellated, accoutrements, hallucination, abrasion, ricochet, surveillance, naive, encore, prestige.

TEST QUESTIONS — No. 5.

Arithmetic. — (1) What kind of money would express the face value of a draft on a bank in Great Britain; in France; in Belgium; in Switzerland; in Austria?

(2) If when I buy goods the seller allows me a discount of 20%, and 15% off for cash, how much cash must I pay for a bill amounting to $450?

(3) A well 3 feet in diameter has 10 feet of water in it. What is the weight of the water? (A cubic foot of water weighs $62\frac{1}{2}$ pounds.)

(4) What per cent. of an acre is a lot 125 feet long and 25 feet wide?

(5) A teacher receives $40 per month for nine months. His board costs him $3 per week; books, association, and institute expenses, $30. What per cent. are his total expenses of his total wages.

Language and Grammar. — (1) Give three nouns which denote plurality, but which have no plural termination.

(2) Which is correct, the *Misses Smith*, or the *Miss Smiths?*

(3) Correct the following, and give reasons: "He

is an alumni of Harvard;" "I had ought to go;" "There is no doubt but what it will rain."

(4) Why is it wrong to use slang?

(5) How many words are in the English language? What author has used the greatest number of different words?

Geography.—(1) Name the seaport of each of the following-named cities: Peking, Lima, Santiago, Paris.

(2) What are trade winds, anti-trade winds, and monsoons?

(3) What causes waterspouts?

(4) A country about the size of Maryland occupies a delta, has a population of between four and five millions, and an immense foreign commerce. Name the country, and its principal cities.

(5) Where is the zone of calms, and what causes it?

United States History.—(1) Name all the Presidents of the United States who were lawyers.

(2) What did the free soil party advocate? How long did the party last?

(3) A certain man sat in the house of representatives and United States senate as a democrat; afterwards sat in the senate as a republican. He was vice president of the United States and minister to Spain. Name him.

(4) A certain man served in the house of representatives; was postmaster general, and associate justice of the supreme court of the United States. Name him, and state what connection he had with an important decision of the court.

(5) What was the X. Y. Z. mission?

General Information.—(1) What is meant by the "postal union"?

(2) What is meant by "rider" in legislation?

(3) What island has two republics? Name them.

(4) What is meant by "subsidy"? Give an illustration.

(5) When was the bureau of education established? Describe briefly its work.

(6) What is the difference between a government *de facto* and a government *de jure?*

(7) Name the author of each of the following-named works: "Citizen of the World," "Society and Solitude," "Jersusalem Delivered," "The Stones of Venice," "Hudibras."

(8) What is the Rosetta stone?

(9) Why was Cleopatra's needle so called?

(10) What is meant by international law?

ANSWERS TO TEST QUESTIONS
No. 5.

Arithmetic.—(1) Pounds; francs; francs; francs; florins.

(2) \$450 less 20 % = \$360.   15 % of \$360 = \$54. \$360 — \$54 = \$306.

(3) Radius is 1.5 ft.   Area of bottom of well is $3.1416 \times (1.5)^2$; $3.1416 \times 2.25 = 7.0686$ sq. ft. Cubic feet of water is $7.0686 \times 10 = 70.686$. Weight of water is $70.686 \times 62\frac{1}{2} = 4417.875$ lbs.

(4) There are 43560 sq. ft. in an acre.   In the lot required there are $125 \times 25 = 3125$ sq. ft.   3125 sq. ft. is 7 + % of 43560 sq. ft.   Hence, the lot is 7 + % of an acre.

(5) Total earnings = \$360.   Total expenses = \$138.   \$138 is $38\frac{1}{3}$ % of \$360.

Language and Grammar.—(1) Cavalry, infantry, cattle.

(2) Authorities conflict. The latter form is sanctioned by the highest authority.

(3) "He is an alumnus of Harvard." *Alumni* is plural. "I ought to go." *Ought* is a defective verb, and has no participle with which to form the perfect tense. "There is no doubt but it will rain." *But what* is a barbarism.

(4) *Slang* is not in accordance with good use. It introduces confusion and barbarism.

(5) Probably over 100,000. Shakespeare, who uses 15,000.

———

Geography.—(1) Peking, Tientsin; Lima, Callao; Santiago, Valparaiso; Paris, Havre.

(2) Winds in the torrid zone, and often a little beyond it, which blow from the same quarter throughout the year, except when affected by local causes; so called because of their usefulness to navigators, and, hence, to trade. They are caused by the joint effect of the rotation of the earth and the movement of the air from the polar to the equatorial regions to supply the vacancy caused by heating, rarefaction, and consequent ascent of the air in the latter regions. Their general direction on the north side of the equator is from northeast to southwest, and from southeast to northwest on the south side of the equator. (*b*) Are found in temperate latitudes. They blow from the southwest in the north temperate, and from the northwest in the south temperate zone. They are separated from the trade winds by the *calms of cancer* and the *calms of capricorn*. (*c*) Winds which blow half the year in one direction, and the other half in an opposite direction. They usually prevail on the western and southern coasts of continents.

(3) Is formed by a tornado passing over a body of water. Waterspouts are most prevalent on the ocean.

(4) Holland.   Amsterdam, Haarlem, Leyden, The
Hague, Rotterdam, Utrecht.

(5) The equatorial belt of calms and rains lies en-
tirely to the north of the equator.   It is caused by
the trades blowing in opposite directions, north and
south of the equator.   It lies north of the line, on
account of the heating influence of the greater mass
of land in the northern hemisphere.

United States History.—(1) John Adams, Thomas
Jefferson, John Quincy Adams, Andrew Jackson,
Martin Van Buren, John Tyler, James K. Polk,
Millard Fillmore, Franklin Pierce, James Buchanan,
Abraham Lincoln, Rutherford B. Hayes, James A.
Garfield, Chester A. Arthur, Grover Cleveland, Ben-
jamin Harrison.

NOTE.—Jas. Madison and Jas. Monroe were law students.

(2) The obligation of Congress to confine slavery
to the slave states, and to refuse its admission into
the territories.   From 1848 to 1856.

(3) Hannibal Hamlin.

(4) John McLean.   He wrote the dissenting opinion in the "Dred Scott" case, in which he held that
slavery had its origin in force, not in right; nor in
general law, to which it is opposed, but in local law,
which cannot be respected by national courts.

(5) The X. Y. Z. letters were written to the United
States commissioners to negotiate a treaty with France
by men who styled themselves X., Y., and Z., pro-

posing to exact a loan from the United States as the price of peace with France. These men acted under instructions from the French minister, Tallyrand, who lied to save himself from the infamy of the transaction. Pinckney, one of the commissioners, is said to have replied to the corruptors: "Millions for defense—not a cent for tribute." The language he did use was not so bombastic, but it meant the same. The X. Y. Z. mission, as it was called, failed in 1798, during John Adams's administration, and almost precipitated a war with France.

General Information.—(1) A union for postal purposes, entered into by the most important powers or governments, such as England, France, Germany, United States, etc., which have agreed to transport mail matter through their respective territories at a stipulated price or rate.

(2) A "rider" is an additional clause annexed to a bill while in course of passing, generally imposing something extra or burdensome upon the measure which could not be enacted into a law if standing upon its own merits.

(3) The island of Hayti. The republics of Hayti and San Domingo.

(4) In international law, a subsidy is a sum of money paid by one sovereign or nation to another to purchase the coöperation or the neutrality of such sovereign or nation in war. England subsidized Austria to join the coalition against Napoleon in 1812,

by an offer of £10,000,000 sterling, and Napoleon had previously subsidized Prussia in 1804, by tempting that nation with the possession of Hanover.

(5) In 1867, "a department of education" was established at Washington, for the purpose of collecting statistics showing the condition and progress of education in the states and territories, and for diffusing such information as might promote the cause of education throughout the country. Congress changed this to "the office of education" in 1868, and made it a part of the department of the interior. The chief officer is styled the commissioner of education. The present commissioner is Dr. W. T. Harris.

(6) A government *de facto* is a government in fact, without regard to whether it is a legal or rightful government. A government *de jure* is one which is supported by law. Thus, during the revolution, Congress was the government *de facto* of the colonies, while England was the government *de jure*. When England recognized the independence of the colonies, Congress became the government *de jure* as well as *de facto*.

(7) Goldsmith, Ralph W. Emerson, Tasso, Ruskin, Butler.

(8) A stone found at Rosetta, in England, containing a trilingual inscription, by which, together with other inscriptions, a key was found by the use of which the hieroglyphics of Egypt are deciphered.

(9) Each of two rose-colored syenite obelisks,

standing near the site of Alexandria, Egypt, for 2,000 years, bears this name. It is not known why they were so called, because they were originally erected at Heliopolis, probably during the reign of Rameses II. It is thought the name may be derived from the fact that the Romans placed them near Alexandria in the reign of Cleopatra. One of these obelisks was presented by the khedive of Egypt to England, and was removed to the bank of the Thames; the other was given to the United States, and now stands in Central park, New York.

(10) Rules governing international intercourse, drawn from usage, diplomatic discussions, text-books, and treaties.

PRONOUNCING CONTEST— No. 5.

Fiancée, carotid, accompaniment, abysmal, caseous, dynamo, heigh-ho, medicament, orchid, recipe, basalt, parabola, tonsilitis, ribald, zodiacal, ibid, anchovy, herculean, trachea, liniment, lineament.

TEST QUESTIONS — No. 6.

Arithmetic.—(1) If my plow cuts 18 inches wide, how many times must I plow around a circular quarter-section to plow one-half of it?

(2) In a two-thirds pitch roof, what is the length of the rafters, if the building is 36 feet wide?

(3) What rate per cent. does a bank make on its money by loaning it on 90-day paper?

(4) What is an annuity?

(5) What is the metric system?

Language and Grammar.—(1) What is meant by *strong* and *weak* verbs?

(2) Write the plural for 9, +, a, box, calf, ox, mouse, manservant, memorandum, money.

(3) Distinguish between the two figures of speech, *metaphor* and *simile.*

(4) Can *perfect, full* and *round* be compared? Reason for answer.

(5) Which of these expressions is correct: "I will see you again, and your hearts shall rejoice." *¿* "I shall see you again, and your hearts will rejoice."

Geography.—(1) How does the domestic commerce of the United States compare with its foreign commerce?

(2) How is the District of Columbia governed?

(3) Explain "standard time."

(4) What constitutes the empire of Japan?

(5) What and where is the lowest land of the earth's surface?

United States History.—(1) For what public act was George Washington so censured that he declared "he would rather be in his grave than in the presidency"? Explain that measure.

(2) What was the *"gunboat system"?* Who was its author?

(3) What and when was the *"era of good feeling"?*

(4) What was done by the *"Poland committee"?* by the *"Potter committee"?*

(5) What are the chief provisions of the interstate commerce act?

(6) What is a "bill of rights"?

(7) Was Andrew Johnson impeached? Reason for answer.

(8) What are the sole powers of the house of representatives?

(9) Give the name and address of each member of Congress from the state of Kansas.

(10) What is the highest office ever held by a Kansas man? Did more than one Kansan ever hold that office? Name him or them.

General Information.—(1) What is the civil day? When did the day begin for the Puritans?

(2) What is the origin of each of the following phrases: "Little Church Around the Corner," "Little Corporal," "Little Giant," "Little Go," "Little Mac," "Little Rhody."

(3) A literary character composed the following enigma:

> " We are little airy creatures,
> All of different voice and features;
> One of us in glass is set,
> One of us you 'll find in jot,
> T' other you may see in tin,
> And the fourth a box within.
> If the fifth you should pursue,
> It can never fly from you."

What is the author's name? Give title to his greatest work. Solve the enigma.

(4) Point out the distinction between a college and a university. Where are the following-named institutions situated: Yale, Leyden, Harvard, Glasgow, Oxford, Berlin, Cambridge, Johns Hopkins. Which are colleges? Which universities? State an interesting fact connected with each.

(5) What is a *wedge* verse?

(6) What is a "*red-letter day*"?

(7) What is the origin of "*In hoc signo vinces*"?

(8) What is the *middle kingdom?*

(9) Who was the *mistress of the Adriatic?*

(10) What is wrong with this quotation from Coleridge's "Ancient Mariner":

> "Clomb above the eastern bar
> The hornèd moon, with one bright star
> Within the nether tip."

ANSWERS TO TEST QUESTIONS
No. 6.

Arithmetic.—(1) 160 acres $= 160 \times 160 = 25,600$ sq. rds. $=$ area.

$\sqrt{25,600 \div 3.1416} = 90.2+$ rds., radius of field. $\frac{1}{2}$ of 160 acres $= 80$ acres $=$ remainder in circular form. 80 acres $= 12,800$ sq. rds. $\sqrt{12,800 \div 3.1416} = 63.8 =$ radius of remainder. $90.2 - 63.8 = 26.4$ rds., width of part plowed. 26.4 rds. $= 5,227.2$ in. $5,227.2 \div 18 = 290.4$, number of times plowed around.

(2) Height of pitch is $\frac{2}{3}$ of $36 = 24$ ft. Then we have a right-angled triangle with 24 ft. for perpendicular, $\frac{1}{2}$ width of house for base (18 ft.), and the rafter for hypotenuse.

$\sqrt{(24)^2 + (12)^2} = 30$, length of rafter from wall of house to top of roof.

(3) By interest tables, the interest on $1 for 93 days at 6 % = 2 cents. Then the bank makes 2 cents on 98 cents in each 93 days, or 8 % yearly.

(4) A sum of money to be paid annually or at stated intervals of time.

(5) A system of weights and measures based upon a unit called a meter, which is one ten-millionth part of the distance from the equator to either pole measured on the earth's surface at the level of the sea.

It was first devised and adopted in France; but is now used in many countries, especially in scientific laboratory work.

Language and Grammar.—(1) *Weak* verbs are those which form the past indicative and the participle by adding *ed* to the present: move, moved, moved. *Strong* verbs undergo a radical change in form to express change in principal parts: go, went, gone.

(2) 9's, +'s, a's, boxes, calves, oxen, mice, menservants, memoranda (or memorandums), moneys.

(3) Metaphor institutes comparison by using the like thing for the thing with which it is compared:

"Now is the winter of our discontent made glorious summer."

(3) *Simile* states the comparison by words expressing the resemblance. "Concealment like a worm i' the bud." In the following, *metaphor* and *simile* are combined:

"I have ventured,
Like little wanton boys that swim on bladders,
These many summers in a sea of glory."

(4) Yes. Language is but the expression of limited͑ human thought and achievement. *Humanly* speaking, a *round* thing may be made *rounder;* a *perfect* thing, *more perfect;* and a *full* thing, *fuller.*

(5) The first expresses determination and obligation; the second, futurity. If you wish, then, to express determination, use the former; if futurity, the latter.

_____

Geography.—(1) The former is about seven times greater than the latter.

(2) By Congress.

(3) Civil time, established by law or usage over a region or country. In England, it is Greenwich. In the United States, four standards have been adopted by the railroads and accepted by the people. These are the mean local times of the 75th, 90th, 105th, and 120th meridians west of Greenwich. These times, beginning with the 75th, are called eastern, central, mountain, and Pacific, respectively, and are five, six, seven and eight hours slower than Greenwich time.

(4) A large number of islands.

(5) The Dead sea, in Palestine, 1,300 feet below sea level.

_____

United States History.—(1) For signing Jay's treaty with England. It was a treaty made by John Jay to avoid war with England. It secured much-needed peace to the United States; but it left England free to impress American seamen, and shut America out of the West India trade.

(2) It was a plan proposed by Thomas Jefferson to build a large number of small gunboats to protect American commerce against the depredations of England. He advocated the use of the gunboats as being more economical than men-of-war.

(3) After the war of 1812, until J. Q. Adams's administration, there was but one political party, the republican; hence the period is called the "Era of Good Feeling."

(4) (a) It investigated the transactions by which the "Credit Mobilier," a corporation organized to contract for the building of the Union Pacific railroad, had corruptly tampered with members of Congress. So called from its chairman, L. P. Poland, of Vermont. The committee, on the 18th of February, 1873, recommended the expulsion of Oakes Ames, of Massachusetts, for bribery, and of James Brooks, of New York, for accepting bribes. The house modified the expulsion into a vote of absolute condemnation. Both men died within three months afterward. (b) It investigated the alleged frauds during the election of 1876 in many states. It unexpectedly unearthed the "cypher telegrams," sent by persons very closely related to Mr. Samuel J. Tilden, which attempted to corrupt certain election returning boards. It was named from C. N. Potter, its chairman.

(5) Appointment of five members of a commission, which shall regulate the commerce between the states, prevent discrimination in rates, the pooling of freights by different roads, and the dividing of earnings amongst different roads.

(6) A statement of personal rights and privileges guaranteed to citizens by the fundamental laws of the state.

(7) Yes. Impeached means accused and held for trial. He was impeached, but not convicted.

(8) To judge of the qualifications of its own members; to make its own rules and regulations; to impeach officers of the government; to originate bills for revenue; to choose its own officers; to choose the President, in event of electoral college failing to choose; to compel the attendance of its members and punish for contempt; to expel members.

(9) John Martin, senator, Topeka.
W. A. Peffer, senator, Topeka.

REPRESENTATIVES.

Case Broderick, First district, Holton.
H. L. Moore, Second district, Lawrence.
T. J. Hudson, Third district, Fredonia.
Charles Curtis, Fourth district, Topeka.
John Davis, Fifth district, Junction City.
Wm. Baker, Sixth district, Lincoln.
Jerry Simpson, Seventh district, Medicine Lodge.
W. A. Harris, Congressman at large, Linwood.

(10) (*a*) President of the senate. (*b*) No. (*c*)
John James Ingalls.

General Information.—(1) (*a*) The period of time
recognized by law as comprised within the word
"day." With us it extends from midnight to midnight. (*b*) At 6 o'clock in the afternoon.

(2) "Little Church Around the Corner:" George
Holland, an actor, died in 1870. The first clergy-
man to whom the family applied refused to bury him,
because of his "sinful business." He told them, however, to go to "the little church around the corner."
They did so, and the rector, Doctor Houghton, con-
sented. The occurrence made the church very popular, and an instrument of great good. The church
is the Church of the Transfiguration, in Twenty-
ninth street, New York. It is a Protestant Episcopal
society. "Little Corporal:" A title of endearment
given to Napoleon Bonaparte by his soldiers after
the battle of Lodi. He was, at that time, small and
slender. "Little Giant:" A name given to Stephen
A. Douglas, because of his small stature associated
with his great intellect. "Little Go:" A public examination in Cambridge University, which is so
called because it is held early in the course, and is
neither so strict nor searching as is the final examination. "Little Mac:" A familiar title given to
Gen. George B. McClellan by his admiring soldiers.
It was used as a political *sobriquet* for him during
the presidential contest of 1864. "Little Rhody:"

Nickname for Rhode Island, the smallest state in the union.

(3) (a) Jonathan (Dean) · Swift. (b) Gulliver's Travels. (c) The vowels, a, e, i, o, and u.

(4) "A college is a society of scholars or friends of learning, incorporated for study or instruction, especially in higher branches of learning."

"A university is an institution organized and incorporated for the purpose of imparting instruction, examining students, and otherwise promoting education in the higher branches of literature, science, art, etc., and empowered to confer degrees in the several arts and faculties, as in theology, law, medicine, music, etc. A university may exist without having any college connected with it, or it may consist of but one college, or it may comprise an assemblage of colleges, established in any place, with professors for instructing students in the sciences and other branches of learning."— *Webster's International Dictionary.*

Yale.—New Haven, Conn., lately was changed in name from a college to a university.

Leyden.—Leyden, Holland, instituted to commemorate the heroic defense of the city in the sixteenth century, in the struggle for independence.

Harvard.—Cambridge, Mass., first college established in America. Supported for a time by tuitions paid "in kind," that is, corn, potatoes, or other farm products.

Glasgow.—Glasgow, Scotland, noted for the great

men who have been its lord rector from time to time. Carlyle was one of them.

Oxford.— Oxford, England, the great school in England for tories.

Berlin.—Berlin, Germany, is the youngest, but most influential, of Prussian universities, and, next to Leipsic, stands at the head of German universities.

Cambridge.—Cambridge, England, one of the oldest and most renowned educational institutions of the English. It occupies the same relation to the whigs and radicals that Oxford does to the conservatives and tories.

Johns Hopkins.—Baltimore, Md., the most noted university in the United States, whose students engage in original investigations.

All are universities.

(5) A verse in which each succeeding word has more syllables than has the word preceding it:

"Hope ever solaces miserable individuals."

(6) It is a fortunate day. It was an ancient custom to mark holidays on calendars in red ink. In church calendars the saints' days are still so marked, and in the Episcopal prayer book saints' days frequently are designated by red-ink letters; hence the name "rubric."

(7) Constantine the Great is said to have seen this motto accompanying the monogram XP in the sky. The XP are the first two letters of the Greek word translated Christ. He adopted the monogram for his standard.

(8) China.

(9) Venice.

(10) The *horned* moon never appears in the east.

PRONOUNCING CONTEST—No. 6.

Project (noun), project (verb), permit (verb), permit (noun), apropos, cheer, abstract, exhaust, literature, suspicion, pronunciation, debt, sear, seer, tack, tact, gin, feint, sluice, slough.

TEST QUESTIONS — No. 7.

Arithmetic.—(1) Find the area of a square field whose diagonal is 8.284 rods longer than its side.

(2) How many sq. yds. of cloth will make a conical tent 10 ft. in diameter and 12 ft. high.

(3) Find the value of: $15 + 9 \div 3 - 2 \times 3$.

(4) My U. S. 5's yield 7 per cent. At what discount were they bought?

(5) I bought a lot for $100 on a credit of six months, and sold it at once for $200 cash. What did I gain, money being worth 6 per cent.?

Language and Grammar.—(1) Define foot, meter and rhyme, as used in prosody.

(2) What is the plural of temperance, scales, deer, species?

(3) Correct such of the following as are incorrect, and give reasons for correction:

(*a*) Let everyone attend to their work.

(*b*) I knew it to be he.

(*c*) It is him whom you saw.

(*d*) I saw him entering the gate and ring the bell.

(*e*) You is the second person.

(4) Conjugate "go" in the present subjunctive.

(5) Write the possessives, plural and singular, of woman, fox, sheep, turkey, lady, it, she, I, and which.

Geography.—(1) Where are days and nights always of equal length?

(2) Why is the climate of northern Europe warmer than that of North America in the same latitude?

(3) There are 10 seas in and around Europe. Name them.

(4) Name and locate the five largest cities in the United States.

(5) Give the boundaries of the United States in degrees of latitude and longitude.

United States History.—(1) How and where did England acquire Canada?

(2) What led to the colonization of Rhode Island?

(3) How were the colonies governed during the revolution?

(4) What armies were engaged in the battles of Antietam, Stone River, and Gettysburg? Who were the generals? Who were victors?

(5) What association have the following phrases with our history: "Tippecanoe and Tyler too," "Old

Hickory," "Young Hickory," "54-40 or fight," "Unconditional Surrender."

General Information.—(1) Name the "Lake Poets." Why so called?

(2) Where is the "Land of inverted order"? Explain the phrase.

(3) Give the origin of the term "lynch law."

(4) Where is the best prose description of "man" in secular literature? Reproduce the description.

(5) Is there such a thing as the "music of the spheres"? Explain the myth.

(6) What nations protect authors by copyright for all time?

(7) Who was the author of "Ça ira," the refrain of the French revolutionary air?

ANSWERS TO TEST QUESTIONS

No. 7.

Arithmetic.—(1) Since the field is square, the sides are of equal length, and the diagonal separates the field into two right-angled triangles. Taking one of these triangles, we have the hypotenuse (8.284 rods) given to find its area. Let the letter a represent the length of each of the sides (base and altitude).

Then $\sqrt{a^2 + a^2} = a\sqrt{2} = 1.4142 \times a$. By conditions given, $1.4142a - a = 8.284$ rods, or $.4142a = 8.284$ rods. Then $a = \frac{8.284}{.4142}$ rods $= 20$ rods, one side. The area is equal to base multiplied by altitude. 20^2 rods $= 400$ sq. rods, or $400 \div 160 = 2\frac{1}{2}$ acres, area of field.

(2) Slant height of cone $= \sqrt{12^2 + 5^2} = 13$. Half slant height $= 6.5$ feet. Circumference of base $= 10 \times 3.1416 = 31.416$ feet. Then, $31.416 \times 6.5 = 204.204$ sq. ft. $= 22.689$ sq. yds.

(3) Multiplication and division must be performed first. $15 + (9 \div 3) - (2 \times 3) = 15 + 3 - 6 = 12$.

(4) A U. S. 5% bond draws $5 yearly. Then, $5 = 7\%$ of cost. 100% of cost $= \frac{100}{7}$ of $5 = \$71\frac{3}{7}$. $\$100 - \$71\frac{3}{7} = \$28\frac{4}{7}$, the discount. $\$28\frac{4}{7} \div 100 = 28\frac{4}{7}\%$, the rate of discount.

(5) Four solutions. First solution: $200 - \$100 = $ part of gain. 3% of $100 = \$3$, which is a gain in interest. Hence, $103 is the gain. Second solution: $100 + $ interest of $200 for six months at 6% $= \$106$. Third solution: If I do not pay interest on $100 for six months I gain: $\$100 \div 1.03 = \$97.087$, present worth. $\$200 - \$97.087 = \$102.913$. Fourth solution: I set apart $100 of the $200 received to meet my payment at the close of the six months. Then, $100 is my gain.

Language and Grammar.—(1) (a) A division of a verse in poetry, consisting of syllables combined

according to accent. (*b*) Meter is the arrangement
of a certain number of feet in a verse. (*c*) Rhyme
is that kind of poetry in which there is a correspondence of sound in the last syllable of two or more
verses.

(2) (*a*) Has no plural. (*b*) Plural form; has no
singular. (*c* and *d*) Same form in both numbers.

(3) (*a*) "Let everyone attend to his work." Singular antecedent, "everyone," requires singular pronoun, "his." (*b*) "I knew it to be him." Pronoun is
object of the verb "knew," and should have objective
form. (*c*) "It is he whom you saw." Pronoun is
predicate of sentence, and should have nominative
form. (*d*) "I saw him enter the gate and ring the
bell." Coördinate constructions should have the same
verb form. (*e*) "You" is not *the* second person. It
is simply *of* the second person; that is, "you" is a
form of the second person.

(4) If I go.   If we go.
    If you go.   If you go.
    If he go.   If they go.

The third person singular is the only distinctive
subjunctive form in the present subjunctive.

(5)
SINGULAR.	PLURAL.	SINGULAR.	PLURAL.
Woman's.	women's.	lady's.	ladies'.
fox's.	foxes'.	its.	theirs or their.
sheep's.	sheep's.	hers or her.	theirs or their.
turkey's.	turkeys'.	whose.	whose.

Geography.—(1) At the equator.

(2) Because of the Gulf Stream, which almost washes the shores of northern Europe.

(3) White, Caspian, Black, Marmora, Archipelago, Adriatic, Mediterranean, Irish, North, Baltic.

(4) Census of 1890: New York, N.Y., 1,515,301; Chicago, Ill., 1,099,850; Philadelphia, Pa., 1,046,964; Brooklyn, N. Y., 806,343; St. Louis, Mo., 451,770.

(5) Main territory of United States: Latitude, 24° 20′ N. to 49° 10′ N. at the Lake of the Woods; longitude, 66° 56′ 48″ W. to 124° 30′ W. from Greenwich. Alaska: Latitude, 52° 2′ N. to 71° 27′ N.; longitude, about 131° W. to 167° E. from Greenwich.

United States History.—(1) By the French and Indian war. The treaty at the close of the war in 1763 ceded Canada to England.

(2) The flight of Roger Williams from Salem because of his religious belief.

(3) By Congress.

(4) (*a*) The union and rebel armies were the combatants in all three. (*b*) Antietam: Federal, George B. McClellan; rebel, Robert E. Lee. Stone River or Murfreesboro: Federal, W. S. Rosecrans; rebel, Braxton Bragg. Gettysburg: Federal, George G. Meade; rebel, Robert E. Lee. (*c*) The union army was victorious in each conflict.

(5) (*a*) It was the campaign cry of the whig party in 1840, and referred to their nominees for the presidency and vice presidency, William Henry Harrison, the victor in the battle of Tippecanoe, during the Indian war of 1811, and John Tyler. (*b*) A sobriquet of Andrew Jackson, suggested by his unbending disposition and powers of endurance. (*c*) Applied to Pres. James K. Polk, who came from Tennessee, the state in which Andrew Jackson lived. (*d*) The alternative war cry of the democratic party in 1845, meaning the northern boundary between the United States and British America should be 54° 40′ north latitude, or there would be war. Wiser heads prevailed, and compromise treaty in 1846 fixed the boundary at the forty-ninth parallel. (*e*) A name applied to General Grant, from the phrase, "unconditional surrender," which occurred in his short, terse reply to General Buckner's proposition for terms to capitulate Fort Donelson.

———

General Information.—(1) (*a*) Wordsworth, Coleridge, and Southey. (*b*) From their place of residence, near the lakes of Cumberland.

(2) (*a*) Australia. (*b*) On account of its peculiar plants and animals. For a delightfully humorous description of them, see Sydney Smith's "Essays."

(3) Summary justice at the hands of a mob. Dates back to revolutionary times, when Charles Lynch, Robert Adams and Thomas Calloway organized an informal court in Virginia, to protect society and

punish outlaws and traitors. They never, however, inflicted the death penalty. Their punishments included flogging, hanging by the thumbs, banishment, etc.

(4) (*a*) Shakespeare's Hamlet, act 2, scene 2. (*b*) "What a piece of work is a man! How noble in reason! how infinite in faculty! in form and moving how express and admirable! in action how like an angel! in apprehension how like a god!"

(5) (*a*) No. (*b*) The disciples of Pythagoras imported the idea into Europe from Asia. According to their belief, the "seven wandering stars," Mercury, Venus, Mars, Jupiter, Saturn, the Sun, and Moon, were each attuned to a note in the harmonic scale, and sounded in accord as they moved through space.

(6) Mexico, Guatemala, and Venezuela.

(7) Benjamin Franklin.

PRONOUNCING CONTEST—No. 7.

Trosseau, fuchsia, conscionable, exhilarate, souvenir, abstemious, precocious, lacquer, cuirass, sough, connoisseur, silhouette, bivouac, reveille, omniscient, ptarmigan, sacerdotal, verdigris, surreptitious, régime.

TEST QUESTIONS — No. 8.

Arithmetic.—(1) The product of two numbers is 117, and their quotient is 1.4. Find the numbers.

(2) Prove the following to be unsolvable: Find the area of a triangle whose sides are 9, 14 and 5 rods.

(3) A triangular field, whose sides are 40, 50 and 60 rods respectively, has a fence built from the middle point of the 50-rod side to the middle point of the 60-rod side. How long is the fence?

(4) One hundred and thirty-five men agree to donate all the money that could be raised by the first man paying one cent, the second two cents, the third three cents, etc., to a charitable institution. How much was raised?

(5) A certain number divided by 11 leaves a remainder of 9; divided by 9, leaves a remainder of 6; by 7, leaves a remainder of 5; by 5, leaves a remainder of 4. What is the number?

Grammar.—(1) Write the synopses of *have, be* and *do* in the first person, singular, indicative.

(2) Give an example of the regular comparison of an adjective; of the irregular.

(3) Can you name one each of the different parts of speech that occur in this question? Do so.

(4) Write a sentence containing a pronoun used as an attribute; as an appositive.

(5) Write a sentence whose subject is modified by a word, a phrase, and a clause.

Geography.—(1) Name four great races of men, and a country in which each is the ruling race.

(2) Locate Fortress Monroe, Corea, Herat, Sydney, Terra del Fuego.

(3) (*a*) In what direction from the tropic of Cancer is the tropic of Capricorn? (*b*) How far?

(4) Through what countries does the Arctic circle pass?

(5) Name three food products exported in large quantities from the United States.

United States History.—(1) What two things, at least, were settled by the civil war?

(2) What President of the United States learned to write after he was married? Who was his teacher?

(3) Who were the "carpetbaggers"?

(4) What was the "Mafia" difficulty in New Orleans?

(5) What is the "Chinese exclusion act"?

General Information.—(1) What is the cause of the present difficulty between China and Japan?

(2) Why are the following phrases of general interest in Kansas this summer: "16 to 1," "woman suffrage," "Wilson bill," "McKinley bill"?

(3) Is there more than one "No Man's Land" in the United States? Give history.

(4) What literary man proposed a "ninth beatitude"? Give text of the proposed blessing.

(5) Who wrote the following: "Maud," "Evangeline," "Snow Bound," "Thanatopsis," "The Spy," "The Legend of Sleepy Hollow," "The Washerwoman's Song," "The Story of a Country Town," "A Kansan Abroad," "Blue Grass"?

ANSWERS TO TEST QUESTIONS

No. 8.

Arithmetic.—(1) The product of two numbers, divided by the quotient of the less into the greater, is equal to the square of the less.

$117 \div 1.\dot{4} = 81$, square of less.

$\sqrt{81} = 9$, less number.

$9 \times 1.\dot{4} = 13$, greater number.

(2) They cannot form a triangle, since one side (14) is as long as the other two (9 + 5). Any one side of a triangle is less than the sum of the other

two sides. It may be proved in another way: The area of a triangle is equal to the continued product of the half sum of the sides and the several remainders obtained by subtracting each side separately from the half sum:

$$9 + 5 + 14 = 28, \text{ whole sum.}$$
$$28 \div 2 = 14, \text{ half sum.}$$
$$14 - 9 = 5$$
$$14 - 5 = 9$$
$$14 - 14 = 0.$$

Multiplying these remainders and the half sum together, we have: $5 \times 9 \times 0 \times 14 = 0$; consequently, there is no area.

(3) It cuts the sides proportionally, and hence it is parallel to the 40-rod side. Then, since it cuts off half the sides, it must be half as long as the 40-rod side, or 20 rods.

(4) First term is 1; last term is 135; number of terms is 135. To find the sum of the series, multiply half the sum of the first and last terms by the number of terms:

$$\frac{1 + 135}{2} \times 135 = 68 \times 135 = 9180 \text{ cents,}$$
$$\text{or, } \$91.80.$$

(5) $11 + 9 = 20$, the first condition. The least multiple of 11 that contains 9 with a remainder of 4 is 22. Then $20 + 22 = 42$, satisfies the first and second conditions. The next condition must be a multiple of 99, and contain 7 with a remainder of 5. This number is 495. $42 + 495 = 537$, satisfying

first, second and third conditions. Similarly, 537 +
2772 = 3309, the required number.

Grammar.—(1)

	HAVE.	BE.	DO.
Present,	I have.	I am.	I do.
Pres. perf.	I have had.	I have been.	I have done.
Past,	I had.	I was.	I did.
Past perf.	I had had.	I had been.	I had done.
Future,	I shall have.	I shall be.	I shall do.
Fut. perf.	I shall have had.	I shall have been.	I shall have done.

(2) (*a*) Regular: Sweet, sweeter, sweetest; manly,
more manly, most manly. (*b*) Irregular: Much,
more, most.

(3) Yes. "Can name" is a verb; "you" is a
pronoun; "of" is a preposition; "different" is an
adjective; "parts" is a noun.

(4) (*a*) I am he. (*b*) You, you are the guilty one.

(5) Desiring to do good, the brave men, whose
names are here written, volunteered to go.

Geography.—(1) The Caucasian in the United
States of America; the Mongolian in China; the
Ethiopian in Africa; the Malay in Java.

(2) Virginia; a peninsula of northeastern Asia;
a fortified town of Afghanistan; a town of New South
Wales, Australia; a group of islands off the southern
extremity of South America.

(3) (*a*) South. (*b*) 47 degrees of latitude, approximately, 3,243 miles.

(4) Norway, Sweden, Russia in Europe, Russia in Asia, Greenland, touches Iceland, British America, Alaska.

(5) Corn, wheat, beef and pork.

United States History.—(1) The abolition of slavery, and the establishment of national supremacy over states rights.

(2) (*a*) Andrew Johnson. (*b*) His wife.

(3) At the close of the war the ignorant freedmen became the tools of unscrupulous men from other states, who worked upon the prejudices of the negroes and obtained office through their votes. Frequently these adventurers had no more property than could be carried in a carpetbag; hence the name.

(4) The "Mafia" is a secret, oath-bound body of assassins in Italy. Immigrants from that country to this established a branch in the city of New Orleans, and inaugurated a reign of terror by murdering those who sought to bring them to justice. At last a number of them were apprehended and tried. The jury, terrified, it is supposed, by the fate which would befall them from other members of the society not apprehended, should a verdict of guilty be rendered, acquitted them. The citizens of New Orleans rose in riot, and killed the prisoners in jail. This led to much correspondence between Italy and the United States, and for a time war seemed imminent. The diplomacy of James G. Blaine and the size of the United States averted the trouble.

(5) An act passed in 1888 to prevent the immigration of Chinese laborers, who were ruining the rates of wages for all civilized laborers.

General Information. — (1) In relation to the suzerainty of the kingdom of Corea, Japan maintains that Japanese residents are not properly protected in Corea, and she proposed great reforms in government for the Coreans. These reforms the Chinese combated, asserting that Corea is under her protection. Japan's plans would have made her the ruling power instead of China. The immediate cause of the war was, it is claimed by the Japanese, the want of protection to the lives and property of Japanese merchants in Corea, and a violation of Japan's nationality by assassinating political insurrectionists who had taken shelter under and were entitled to the protection of Japan's flag.

(2) (*a*) The ratio at which the government should coin gold and silver. The "silver kings" insist that coinage shall be free at the ratio of 16 parts of silver to one of gold. The "gold bugs" insist the ratio should be higher, ranging from 19 to 28 parts of silver to one of gold. (*b*) An amendment to the constitution extending the general right of suffrage to women is to be voted upon this fall. (*c*) A bill which took its name from Representative Wilson, of West Virginia. It was a bill to reduce the tariff, and looked toward free trade. It never became a law, a compromise between the tariff wing and the free-

trade wing of the democratic party being adopted instead. (*d*) The McKinley bill was a high-protective measure adopted by the republicans, and repealed by the compromise on the Wilson bill above referred to. These two bills and their respective merits bring the whole question of tariff and free trade up for discussion — a question that is always with us.

(3) Yes; there are three such. The first, a long, narrow strip of land lying west of Indian Territory, north of Texas, east of New Mexico, and south of Kansas. None of these had jurisdiction over it; hence the name. It is now incorporated into Oklahoma territory. The second is a strip on the boundary between Pennsylvania and Delaware. The official surveys give it to Pennsylvania; but the people vote in Delaware, and the title deeds to their real estate are recorded in that state. The third is an uninhabited island near Martha's Vineyard, off the Massachusetts coast.

(4) (*a*) Alexander Pope. (*b*) "Blessed is he who expects nothing; for he shall never be disappointed."

(5) Tennyson, Longfellow, Whittier, Bryant, Cooper, Irving, Eugene Ware, Howe, Noble Prentis, John James Ingalls.

PRONOUNCING CONTEST—No. 8.

Subpœna, malleable, pedal, broncho, rigidity, anchovy, leisure, corollary, cosine, gerrymander, ancillary, extraordinary, counsel, consul, refutable, inoculate, farrier, interpolate, mandible, sleight.

TEST QUESTIONS — No. 9.

Arithmetic.—(1) Given the sum and difference of two numbers, how would you find the less?

(2) Where did the Arabic notation originate?

(3) Two-thirds of the cube of a certain number is 10 more than the cube of its two-thirds. What is the number?

(4) I can pick 40 bushels of potatoes or dig 20 bushels in a day. How many bushels can I pick and dig in a week?

(5) I buy a certain article by avoirdupois and sell by apothecaries' weight. Do I make or lose? How much?

Grammar.—(1) Write the possessives of whosoever and whoever.

(2) Distinguish between adjectives — attributive, predicate, and complement. Give examples of each.

(3) Which of the following are correct? which incorrect? Reasons for answers. (*a*) *These* is the plural of *this*. (*b*) "We are agreed," says I. (*c*) Either you or I am going. (*d*) What a beautiful phenomena! (*e*) I knew it to be him.

(4) In regard to language, what is meant by good usage?

(5) From what language are our *strong* verbs derived?

Geography.—(1) Which is longer, the solar or sidereal day? How much? Why?

(2) What is the cause of the earth's revolution?

(3) What and where is the Orange Free State?

(4) How does Japan rank in civilization?

(5) What influence have mountain systems upon the continent to which they belong? Illustrate.

United States His'ory.—(1) In what great American state papers do the following occur: (*a*) "In the name of God, amen." (*b*) "When in the course of human events." (*c*) "We, the people of the United States." (*d*) "Congress shall make no law respecting an establishment of religion." (*e*) "Both read the same Bible, and pray to the same God."

(2) What states came into the union in each of the following years: 1790, 1820, 1850, 1890?

(3) What was the "Quaker policy" of our government?

(4) Who were the "Mugwumps"?

(5) What was the decision of the "Bering sea tribunal"?

General Information.—(1) Who used the phrase, "Let no guilty man escape"? Under what circumstances?

(2) What is the meaning and origin of "O. K."?

(3) Who was the "Old Public Functionary"? Why so called?

(4) Tell the story of "The Great Bottle Hoax"?

(5) Where do these characters figure: Sancho Panza, Salathiel, Tiny Tim, Jennie Dean, Amelia Sedley, Messala, Rasselas, Roger de Coverley, Uncle Tom.

ANSWERS TO TEST QUESTIONS
No. 9.

Arithmetic.—(1) The sum of two numbers less their difference is twice the lesser number.

(2) The characters and the decimal notation came from Hindostan.

(3) Two-thirds of a number cubed $= \frac{8}{27}$ of the cube of the number. The $\frac{2}{3}$ of the cube, $\frac{18}{27}$, $- \frac{8}{27}$ $= \frac{10}{27}$, and $\frac{10}{27} = 10$; whence, $\frac{27}{27} = 27$, the cube of the number. The number then is $\sqrt[3]{27} = 3$.

(4) I can pick twice as many as I can dig; therefore I must dig twice as long as I pick. Then I must dig 4 days and pick 2. $20 \times 4 = 80$ bushels.

(5) You make $17\frac{5}{7}\%$; 1 lb. av. $= 7000$ grs.; 1 lb. ap. $= 5760$ grs. Difference gained is 1240 grs., which is $17\frac{5}{7}\%$ of 7000 grs.

Grammar.—(1) Whosesoever, whoseever.

(2) Attributive adjectives are those which are used to modify nouns directly; as, A *good* man. Adjectives, predicate and complement, are interchangeable terms used to designate adjectives employed to complete predication; as, He is *sick*.

(3) (*a*) Is correct, "these," as here used, being a noun in the singular number. (*b*) Should read "say I." The form of the verb should be first person, singular number. (*c*) Good usage requires that in an alternative between the first and second persons, the verb should agree with the second person rather than with the first. (*d*) "Phenomenon" is the singular form. (*e*) The proper case form for the predicate of a sentence is the nominative, hence "him" should be changed to "he."

(4) The usage of the best writers and speakers.

(5) Anglo-Saxon.

Geography.—(1) (*a*) The solar day. (*b*) About four minutes the longer. (*c*) Because the earth moves forward in its orbit, while it revolves upon its axis, about 1 degree a day (360 degrees in a year). Consequently, when the earth has made a complete revolution, it must perform a part of another revolution through this additional degree in order to bring this same meridian vertically under the sun.

(2) ·The earth's motion is due to motion imparted to it when it was first created. By the law of inertia it would move indefinitely in one direction, but by attraction of the sun it is constantly changing its direction, by falling toward the sun. This imparts the elliptical shape to its orbit.

(3) A Dutch settlement in east South Africa, containing 48,038 square miles, bounded by Natal, Cape Colony, and the Transvaal republic. It has a population of 75,000, one-half Dutch. It is adapted to the raising of cattle and sheep.

(4) The most-highly civilized of Mongolian nations. No nation ever made such rapid advances as has Japan during the last 25 years.

(5) Their cold tops condense the moisture brought from the sea by the winds. This produces rain, which is turned by the conformation of the slopes into rivers.

United States History.—(1) (_a_) The Mayflower compact. (_b_) Declaration of independence. (_c_) Preamble to the constitution of the United States. (_d_) Bill of rights (first 10 amendments to constitution of the United States). (_e_) Abraham Lincoln's second inaugural address, March 4, 1865.

(2) 1790, Rhode Island. 1820, Maine. 1850, California. 1890, Idaho.

(3) An effort made by General Grant, when President, to inaugurate a more humane and a juster treatment of the Indians. It was so called from an announcement made in his first annual message, that he had begun "a new policy toward these wards of the nation, by giving the management of a few reservations of Indians to members of the Society of Friends." The Society of Friends nominated agents to President Grant, and, on his approval, they were appointed. Soon after, other reservations were intrusted to other religious bodies.

(4) The republicans of New York who refused to support James G. Blaine for President in 1884, and elected Grover Cleveland by supporting him.

(5) Against the claim of the United States to exclusive jurisdiction of the seas beyond three miles from shore. Stringent provisions against both England and the United States for the protection of the seals.

———

General Information.—(1) (*a*) General Grant. (*b*) In 1875, when Secretary Bristow was instituting proceedings against members of the "whisky ring," some of whom were close, personal friends of President Grant, the President indorsed upon a letter relating to the prosecutions: "Let no guilty man escape, if it can be avoided. No personal consideration should stand in the way of performing a public duty." The matter leaked out, and the first phrase of the indorsement became a popular cry.

(2) It is said that an ignorant clerk, supposing "all correct" to be spelled "oll korect," used "O. K." as his mark.

(3) President Buchanan so called himself in his message to the last Congress in session before the rebellion of the Southern states.

(4) In 1749, the Duke of Portland and the Earl of Chesterfield, in conversing upon human gullibility, entered into a wager that, if a man should advertise that he would jump into a quart bottle, he would find enough fools in London to fill a playhouse to see him perform the feat, and pay for the opportunity. The Duke of Portland won his wager, but the duped audience looted the house and robbed the till of the manager.

(5) (a) "Adventures of Don Quixote de la Mancha," by Cervantes. (b) "Salathiel, the Wandering Jew," by Eugene Sue. (c) "A Christmas Carol," by Charles Dickens. (d) "Heart of Midlothian," by Walter Scott. (e) "Vanity Fair," by W. M. Thackeray. (f) "Ben-Hur," by Lew. Wallace. (g) "Rasselas," by Samuel Johnson. (h) "The Spectator," by Joseph Addison. (i) "Uncle Tom's Cabin," by Harriet B. Stowe.

PRONOUNCING CONTEST—No. 9.

Inscrutable, combatant, inimical, hautboy, literature, biography, leguminose, indefatigable, ascent,
assent, corporeal, boatswain, medullary, fiduciary,
consignee, lachrymose, gullible, quinsy, tic doulou-
reux, Youghiogheny.

TEST QUESTIONS—No. 10.

Arithmetic.—(1) Upon what five principles is the Roman notation founded?

(2) A load of hay weighs 2,280 pounds. What will it cost at $18.50 per ton?

(3) What two values have figures?

(4) Given the sum and difference of two numbers, how would you find the greater?

(5) Solve by proportion: If a man earn $192 in 8 days by working 6 hours a day, how much can he earn in 20 days by working 10 hours a day?

Grammar.—(1) What are the accidents of nouns?

(2) Write a sentence in which the antecedent of "what" is expressed?

(3) How do you determine whether a verb is transitive or intransitive?

(4) What is an impersonal verb? Illustrate.

(5) What is the distinction between the grammar and the rhetoric of a language?

Geography.—(1) Define the terms earth's aphelion and perihelion?

(2) (a) How many equinoxes? (b) Name them.
(c) Why are they so called?

(3) What zones only have the four seasons?

(4) Name the territories of the United States?

(5) What is the "circle of fire" referred to in the Kansas normal institute course of study for 1894?

United States History.—(1) What great American died September 7, 1894?

(2) Who were the Locofocos? Why so called?

(3) Why is Texas called the "Lone Star State"?

(4) Name the vice presidents who have become Presidents.

(5) What was the "reciprocity measure" connected with the McKinley bill?

General Information.—(1) What is the meaning of "boycott"? How did it get its name?

(2) What is the significance of the phrase "Chiltern hundreds

(3) What are "Aldines" and "Elzevirs"?

(4) What people punish with "forty stripes, save one"? Why?

(5) What was the "hot-water war" in American history?

ANSWERS TO TEST QUESTIONS
No. 10.

Arithmetic.—(1) (*a*) Repeating a letter repeats its value. (*b*) When a letter is placed after one of greater value, the two express a number equal to the sum of their values. (*c*) When a letter is placed before one of greater value, the two express a number equal to the difference of their values. (*d*) When a letter is placed between two, each of greater value, its value is taken from the sum of their values. (*e*) Placing a dash over a letter multiplies its value by 1,000.

(2) 2,280 lbs. $= 1\frac{7}{50}$ ton.

$1\frac{7}{50} \times \$18.50 = \$21.09.$ *Ans.*

(3) Two—simple, and local or representative. Simple is its value in units' place; local, when it changes location, as in tens', hundreds', etc., places.

(4) Add the sum and difference and divide the result by two.

(5) $\begin{array}{l} \text{8 days : 20 days} \\ \text{6 hours : 10 hours} \end{array} :: \$192 : (?)$

$$\frac{\$192 \times 20 \times 10}{6 \times 8} = \$800. \ Ans.$$

Grammar.—(1) Person, number, gender, and case.

(2) I cannot.

(3) By the sense of the sentence in which it is

used. If, upon asking the question what? or whom? the verb requires a noun or substantive meaning a different thing than the subject to complete its meaning, it is transitive; otherwise, intransitive.

(4) One which expresses action or state independently of its subject: It *rains*.

(5) Grammar concerns itself with the correct expression of thought. Rhetoric has to do with the correct and effective expression of thought and feeling.

Geography.—(1) When the earth reaches that portion of its orbit where it is the most remote from the sun, it is in aphelion; where nearest, perihelion.

(2) Two—vernal and autumnal—equinoxes, because the days and nights are equal; vernal, because the sun is on the equator on the 22d of March, or beginning of spring; autumnal, because the sun is on the line the second time on the 22d day of September, or beginning of autumn.

(3) Temperate zones.

(4) Indian, New Mexico, Arizona, Utah (not yet in full statehood), Oklahoma, and Alaska.

(5) The tract of heated soil in the neighborhood of the Caspian sea is sometimes so called. The name is also sometimes used to designate the *aurora borealis*.

United States History.—(1) Oliver Wendell Holmes.

(2) At a democratic convention in New York, in

1835, some person or persons stopped the proceedings of the meeting by suddenly extinguishing the lights. Some of the delegates had matches known as "locofocos" in their pockets, and with these relighted the lamps. From that time, and for about 10 years thereafter, "locofocos" was the common name for democrats in New York state.

(3) In 1836, Texas declared her independence of Mexico. In 1837, she applied for admission into the union, but·no action was taken; and, until she was admitted, some years later, Texas was known as the "Lone Star" state.

(4) Those who became President while serving as vice president were Tyler, Fillmore, Johnson, Arthur. The following-named vice presidents became Presidents by election: John Adams, Thomas Jefferson.

(5) It provided that a special commercial treaty might be made, by which certain imports from the country subscribing to the treaty would be admitted free of duty, in return for a like privilege extended to certain exports from the United States to that country.

General Information.—(1) (a) A combining to withhold or prevent dealings or social intercourse with a tradesman, employer, etc.; social and business interdiction, for the purpose of coercion. (b) Some years ago, in Ireland, a Captain Boycott having become unpopular, laborers refused to work for him, and his neighbors refused to have any dealings with him.

(2) When a member of the British parliament re-signs, he accepts the "Chiltern Hundreds." This is because no member can resign, except to take a pub-lic office. The steward of the "Chiltern Hundreds" was, in old times, appointed by the crown to protect the people of Bucks from the robbers who frequented the Chiltern hills. Of course, there is no necessity for the office now, but it is made use of to enable members of parliament to resign. When one accepts the office, he immediately vacates it to give others a chance.

(3) (a) Editions of the Greek and Latin classics, published by Aldo Manuzio and his son Paolo, in the fifteenth century. Aldo invented the type called "italics," which type was at one time called *aldine*. (b) Editions of classic authors, printed by the Elzevir family.

(4) (a) The Jews. (b) Because 40 was the highest number of stripes allowed to be inflicted by their law, and, for fear of exceeding that number, they gave "40 save 1."

(5) It occurred in 1799, and the field of battle was Pennsylvania. Immediately after the suppression of the "Whisky Rebellion," the national government at-tempted to collect a direct tax on houses. When the officers came to make the necessary measurements, the women resisted them, and drove them away by

deluging them with hot water. Hence the name.
The disturbance came near developing seriously.
One Fries, for making a rescue of parties resisting
the collectors of the tax, was convicted of treason
and condemned to death. He was pardoned by
President Adams. The obnoxious tax was repealed,
two or three years later, during President Jefferson's
administration.

PRONOUNCING CONTEST—No. 10.

Rarity, holocaust, hegira, gourmand, gneiss, finesse,
cylindric, paradigm, terpischorean, wreath, wreathe,
cicerone, caricature, capuchin, chauvinism, hydro-
pathist, long-lived, rationale, catafalque, cacique.

TEST QUESTIONS — No. II.

Arithmetic.—(1) A railroad train is going at the rate of 60 miles an hour. How many feet does it go in $1\frac{1}{2}$ minutes?

(2) Find the length of the side of a square field which contains 100 acres.

(3) Each shovelful of earth thrown out by a laborer excavating a cellar averages two-thirds of a cubic foot of earth. At that rate, how many shovelsful will be required to fill a wagon which holds a cubic yard of earth?

(4) Three counties combined are required to furnish the national army a regiment of soldiers — 1,000 men. The populations of the counties are 65,000, 48,500, and 76,200, respectively. How many men must each county furnish?

(5) The length of the school term in a certain district is 180 days, or 1,080 hours. One of the pupils was absent during the term 35 days, and los', by tardiness, 40 hours. What percentage of the whole time did he lose?

Language and Grammar.—(1) Make sentences in which the following words are used correctly: *Tan-*

gible, adept, tenacious, respectively, indigenous, in-genuous, ingenious, perfidious, pernicious, cynosure.

(2) Give two good reasons why slang should never be used.

(3) Give at least five rules which you should follow in letter writing.

(4) Give an example of *epigram, irony, hyperbole, metaphor, metonymy.*

(5) Give three English words derived from the Celtic, three from the Dutch, three from the French, three from the Italian, three from the Spanish.

Geography.—(1) Name a country in which each of the following-named animals is used as a beast of burden: The llama, yak, camel, elephant, reindeer, dog.

(2) What causes the great difference between the climate of the eastern and western coasts of the United States?

(3) Define the following words: Erosion, fauna, flora, snow line, ethnography.

(4) Name the countries in which the franc is current; the gulden; the milreis; the mark; the piastre.

(5) Name the nations to which the following-named places belong: New Caledonia, Faroe Isles, Azores, New Guinea, Caroline islands.

United States History.—(1) What was the tenure-of-office act?

(2) What was Morgan's raid?

(3) When was the department of the interior established? What is its work?

(4) What is meant in our history as "the right of expatriation"?

(5) Under whose administration was the interstate-commerce act passed? the Washington monument completed? standard time adopted? the temperance crusade? the "salary grab"?

General Information.—(1) How fast do glaciers move?

(2) What made each of the following-named persons celebrated: Haydn, Charles Wolfe, Rouget de Lisle, Comenius, James Wilson?

(3) What is a "blockade" in war?

(4) Give the authors of the expressions, "Knowledge is power;" "God the first garden made, and the first city Cain;" "Not lost, but gone before;" "Men are but children of a larger growth;" "Necessity the mother of invention."

(5) Name the books in which the following names represent characters: Ichabod Crane, Smike, Portia, Dominie Sampson, Doctor Primrose, Miriam, Alfred Jingle, Becky Sharp, Prospero.

ANSWERS TO TEST QUESTIONS
No. II.

Arithmetic.—(1) 60 miles an hour = 1 mile a minute; then in $1\frac{1}{2}$ minutes train will travel $1\frac{1}{2}$ times 1 mile, or $1\frac{1}{2}$ miles.

1 mile = 5,280 ft.

$1\frac{1}{2}$ miles = $\dfrac{5,280 \times 3}{2}$ = 7,920 ft.

(2) Area = length × width.

100 a. = area.

100 a. = 16,000 sq. rd.

16,000 sq. rd. = length × width.

Since length and width are equal in a square, 16,000 sq. rd. = length ^{2}, or width ^{2}.

$\sqrt{16,000}$ = length, or width, or 126.5 rds. nearly.

(3) Cu. yd. = 27 cu. ft. 27 cu. ft. ÷ $\frac{2}{3}$ = shovelfuls. $40\frac{1}{2}$ = shovelfuls.

(4) The figures given would give us a *fraction* of a man for each county. Take instead the number of troops to be furnished as 1,897, instead of 1,000; then the counties would furnish quotas as follows:

$\frac{65000}{189700}$ of 1,897 = 650.

$\frac{48500}{189700}$ of 1,897 = 485.

$\frac{76200}{189700}$ of 1,897 = 762.

(5) 6 hrs. in school day. 6×35, or 210 hrs., in 35 school days. 210 + 40 = 250 lost hrs. 250 is $23\frac{4}{27}\%$ of 1,080 hrs.

Language and Grammar.—(1) That which can be touched is *tangible*. He is an *adept* in flattery. The Scotch are a *tenacious* people. He spoke of them as a, b, and c, *respectively*. Tobacco is *indigenous* to America. A child is more *ingenuous* than is an adult. The inventor is *ingenious*. He is a *perfidious* man. That doctrine is *pernicious*. The man in public life is the *cynosure* of all eyes.

(2) Slang is vulgar, and corrupts the language as well as the individual. It is difficult to understand. Language should be clear, and susceptible of but one meaning.

(3) (*a*) Write the full address plainly at the beginning of the letter. (*b*) Be brief and clear. (*c*) Make a paragraph for the expression of each thought. (*d*) Be sure that no words are misspelled. (*e*) See that your punctuation assists in interpreting your thought. (*f*) Write your address in full at the close. The first and last directions are to secure either the safe delivery or return of the letter should it miscarry.

(4) "A little learning is a dangerous thing."— *Pope.* "A nice man is a man of nasty ideas."— *Swift.* (He intended the reverse.) "Is she not more than painting can express?"—*Rowe.* "He was not merely a chip off the old block, he was the old block itself."—*Burke.* "Martin, if dirt was trumps, what hands you would hold."—*Charles Lamb.*

(5) Celtic—clan, brogue, whisky. Dutch—pa-
troon, boss, stoop. French—levee, crevasse, bayou.
Italian—macaroni, vermicelli, pantaloon. Spanish
—ranche, cañon, stampede.

Geography.—(1) Llama, Peru; yak, India; camel,
Egypt; elephant, India; reindeer, Lapland; dog,
Greenland.

(2) The cold currents of the north Atlantic flow
near the New England coast, while the return warm
current of the Japanese stream flows near the western coast.

(3) Erosion—the wearing away of the earth by
the action of water, air, or other agencies. Fauna—
the animal life of a country is its fauna. Flora—
the name applied to the vegetable life of a section of
the earth. Snow line—the lowest altitude at which
snow falls and lies on the mountain side the year
around. Ethnography—the branch of knowledge
which deals with the characteristics of the human
family, furnishing the details for ethnology.

(4) Franc—France, Belgium, and Switzerland.
Gulden—Holland. Milreis—Portugal. Mark—
Germany. Piastre—Spain, Turkey, and Egypt.

(5) New Caledonia, France; Faroe Isles, Denmark; Azores, Portugal; New Guinea, Germany,
The Netherlands, and Great Britain; Caroline islands, Spain.

United States History.—(1) It was an act passed during the conflict between Congress and President Johnson. It provided that no officer for whose appointment the consent of the senate was needful could be removed without the consent of the senate.

(2) A cavalry raid made by the rebel general John Morgan during the rebellion, in the year 1863, through Kentucky and Ohio.

(3) In 1849. Has charge of internal affairs, and has under its direction more interests than has any other department, including public lands, patent office, pensions, Indians, census, and education.

(4) The right of a man to abjure his allegiance to one country and become a citizen of another country.

(5) (*a*) President Cleveland's first administration. (*b*, *c*) President Arthur's. (*d*, *e*) President Grant's second administration.

General Information.—(1) But a few inches in a day. Some do not exceed a few inches in a month.

(2) Haydn—musical composer. Charles Wolfe wrote "The Burial of Sir John Moore. De Lisle wrote the "Marseillaise." Comenius—author of the first pictorial schoolbook. James Wilson—American jurist and signer of the declaration of independence, and one of the most prominent framers of the United States constitution.

(3) The investment of a port by ships, preventing ingress or egress and the reception of supplies.

(4) Francis Bacon. Abraham Cowley. Copied from Seneca by both Samuel Rogers, in his "Human Life," and Matthew Henry, in his "Commentaries." John Dryden. The same expression occurs in Franck's "Northern Memoirs," written in 1658 and printed in 1694, Wycherly's "Love in a Wood," 1672, and Farquhar's "Twin Rivals," 1705.

(5) Ichabod Crane, "The Legend of Sleepy Hollow. Smike, "Nicholas Nickleby." Portia, "The Merchant of Venice." Dominie Sampson, "Guy Mannering." Doctor Primrose, "The Vicar of Wakefield. Miriam, "The Marble Faun." Alfred Jingle, "The Pickwick Papers." Becky Sharp, "Vanity Fair." Prospero, "The Tempest."

PRONOUNCING CONTEST—No. 11.

Homœopathy, lachrymose, Medina, Paraguay, Kilauea, Kennebec, Synope, worse, wreath, wreathe, genuine, disdain, hollo, hollow, heather, yea, succinct, whorl, whirl, jowl.

TEST QUESTIONS—No. 12.

Arithmetic.—(1) Express the ratio of 2 to 3 in two different ways.

(2) I have a triangular field 6 rods by 7 rods by 9 rods. Find the area, and state the rule.

(3) Which is the larger, a circle having a diameter of 3 feet, or a square with a side of 3 feet? How much larger?

(4) Compare the cubical contents of a cylinder and a cone having heights and diameters equal.

(5) Indicate 4 raised to the fifth power. Indicate the fifth root of 4 to be extracted.

Language and Grammar.—(1) Correct the following: Come and see me. What did you do it for? Is that the gent? She is our washer lady. I reckon it will rain.

(2) Illustrate the proper use of *may* and *can.*

(3) When should parenthesis marks be used?

(4) Classify subordinate conjunctions, giving an example of each class.

(5) What is meant by the agreement of words?

Geography.—(1) What is an avalanche? Mention localities where avalanches are common.

(2) What two monarchies of Europe are absolute?

(3) Give the approximate population of the world; of the United States; of New York state; of Kansas.

(4) Arrange the following-named cities in the order of population, beginning with the largest: Berlin, Pekin, London, Canton, Vienna, New York, Calcutta, Chicago, and Paris.

(5) Write the names of the states admitted to the union since 1875, giving the capital of each.

United States History.—(1) What were the chief points in the compromise of 1850?

(2) Who were the "anti-Nebraska" men?

(3) What was the estimated cost of the war of the rebellion?

(4) What were "wildcat banks," and when were they prominent in our history?

(5) State briefly the provisions of the "presidential succession act" and the "electoral count act."

General Information.—(1) What is the origin of the phrase "higher law"?

(2) Who was the greatest literary forger that ever lived?

(3) What are the correct names for the following *nom de plumes?* Ik Marvel, Charles Egbert Craddock, Boz, Junius, Waverly.

(4) Give the title of the best work, in your opinion, of Byron, Shelley, Goldsmith, Hugo, Goethe, Cervantes, Virgil, Hawthorne, Bryant, and Burns.

(5) Name four good histories of the United States, and give the period covered by each.

ANSWERS TO TEST QUESTIONS

No. 12.

Arithmetic.—(1) 2:3; $\frac{2}{3}$.

(2) $6+7+9=22$. $22 \div 2 = 11$. $11-6=5$; $11-7=4$; $11-9=2$. $\sqrt{5 \times 4 \times 2 \times 11} = \sqrt{440}$, or 20.97 square rods.   When the three sides of a triangle are given, the area is found by taking the square root of the continued product of the half sum of all the sides by the difference between that half sum and each of the respective sides.

(3) Area of square $= 3^2 = 9$ sq. feet.   Area of circle $= 3.1416 \times (\frac{3}{2})^2 = 7.0686$, nearly, sq. feet. The square is larger, by 1.9314 square feet.

(4) A cone is *one-third* of a cylinder having the same base and height.

(5) 4^5, $\sqrt[5]{4}$.

_____

Language and Grammar.—(1) Come to see me. Why did you do it? Is that the gentleman? She is our washerwoman. I suppose (or think) it will rain.

(2) May I go? I can do it.

(3) Whenever an expression is introduced for explanation or amplification in the midst of a sentence, the marks indicate that the main issue is suspended for the introduction of the subordinate or explanatory thought.

(4) They are classified according to the office of the subordinate. *Adjective:* "I looked for a slide where I could climb," etc. *Substantive:* "I did not doubt that I was done." *Adverbial:* "He went on, while I stumbled," etc.

(5) When two words bear certain grammatical relations one to the other, they are said to agree. Thus, substantives must agree with their verbs in number and person by having the same person and number as do the verbs.

_____

Geography.—(1) Accumulated snow which slips down the slopes of high mountains with resistless force. Switzerland and other countries bordering on the Alps.

(2) Russia and Turkey.

(3) (*a*) 1,500,000.   (*b*) 65,000,000.   (*c*) 6,250-
000.   (*d*) 1,400,000.

(4) London, Paris, Pekin, Canton, New York,
Berlin, Vienna, Chicago, Calcutta.

(5) Colorado, capital, Denver; North Dakota,
capital, Bismarck; South Dakota, capital, Pierre;
Montana, capital, Helena; Washington, capital,
Olympia; Idaho, capital, Boise City; Wyoming,
capital, Cheyenne.

United States History.—(1) California to be admitted as a free state; Utah (including Nevada) and
New Mexico (including Arizona) to be organized
without reference to slavery; the slave trade to be
abolished in the District of Columbia; the passing of
a more stringent fugitive slave law.

(2) When, in 1854, the Kansas-Nebraska bill was
passed, virtually repealing the Missouri compromise,
all northern men who were opposed to the further
extension of slavery united under the name of anti-
Nebraska men.   This was the origin of the Republican party.

(3) About eight billions of dollars.

(4) They were banks which sprang up all over the
country during Jackson's last term. These banks
issued bills which they were not able to redeem.
Bills issued in one state would be refused or heavily
discounted in another.   When President Jackson

ordered that payments for public lands (in which at
that time there was a wild speculation) be paid in
specie, people flocked to the banks to exchange bills
for specie. The results were bank failures and the
panic of 1837.

(5) (*a*) It was passed in 1886, and provided that,
in case of the death or disability of both the President and vice president, the succession to the presidency shall be in the following order: Secretary of
state; of the treasury; of war; attorney general;
secretary of the navy; postmaster general; secretary
of the interior. The department of agriculture had
not been instituted at that time. It is a later cre-
ation. It is provided that the member who thus
becomes President shall be known as "acting President," and that he shall serve until the disability is removed or until a new President is elected.
(*b*) It was passed in 1887. It provides for the
settlement of disputes relative to the validity of the
electoral vote from any state by the tribunals of that
state.

_____

General Information.—(1) It was uttered by William H. Seward in a speech delivered on March 11,
1850.

(2) Alcibiades Simonides, born on the island of
Cyrene, 1818; died 1890. He published forgeries
of Homer's writings, the Assyrian tablets, and the
philosophies of the eastern and western Roman em-
pires.

(3) Donald Mitchell, Miss Murfree, Charles Dickens, probably Sir Philip Francis, Sir Walter Scott.

(4) Childe Harold, The Cloud or the Skylark, The Vicar of Wakefield, Les Miserables, Faust, Don Quixote, Æneid, The Scarlet Letter, Thanatopsis, The Cotter's Saturday Night.

(5) Bancroft's brings our history down to the formation of the constitution. Von Holst's Constitutional History of the United States gives our constitutional history from its origin. Hildreth's History (federalist) brings our history down to 1820. Schouler's History (democratic) comes down to the Mexican war. McMaster's History (republican) covers the period from the revolution to the civil war.

PRONOUNCING CONTEST—No. 12.

Converse (verb), converse (noun), converse (adjective), Los Angeles, Munich, pedagogical, pedagogism, palette, idle, idol, idyl, patentee, Philippi, *qui vive*, retributive, supine (noun), supine (adjective), Sabacthani, lorgnette, obligato.

TEST QUESTIONS — No. 13.

Arithmetic.—(1) A railway train leaves Chicago for Kansas City at 6 P. M., and goes at the rate of 3,080 feet per minute. Another train on the same line leaves Kansas City for Chicago at 5 P. M., and goes at the rate of 3,520 feet per minute. If the distance from Chicago to Kansas City is 490 miles, where will the trains pass.

(2) Which will cost the more and how much: to fence a tract of land 50 rods square, or a tract 125 rods long and 20 rods wide? supposing the fencing to cost — cents per rod. Which is the larger field?

(3) On a farm containing 160 acres in the form of a square a ravine averaging 60 rods long and 6 rods wide cannot be cultivated; a public road running along two sides of the farm takes off a width of two rods; and there is a tract of timber land averaging 40 rods long and 15 rods wide. Deducting the number of acres which cannot be cultivated, how much is left?

(4) A telephone pole is 40 feet high. From the top of a post 10 feet high, set perpendicularly at a distance of 20 feet from the foot of the pole, a wire is stretched to the top of the pole. How long is the wire?

(5) In a two-thirds pitch roof, what is the length of the rafters, if the building is 24 feet wide?

Language and Grammar.—(1) Make sentences in which the following words are used correctly: Nefarious, incongruous, discrepancies, exemplary, precedent (verb), precedent (noun), contumely, truculent, contest (verb), contest (noun).

(2) What words are opposite in meaning to the following: Ideal, fact, infinite, proud, zenith, frigid, constant, theist, condemn, progression.

(3) Write sentences containing the word "that" as a noun, pronoun, adjective, conjunction.

(4) What may be the antecedent of a relative pronoun?

(5) Correct the following, and give reasons: "I expect he is sick." "They presented him with a gold-headed cane." "He enthused the meeting." "He died with a fever." "Yours, &c." (at close of a letter).

Geography.—(1) Has Lake Michigan any tide? If so, how much?

(2) Define *field ice, floe, pack ice, drift ice.*

(3) How do you account for the salt deposits in New York, Ontario, and Michigan?

(4) Name the five countries of the world which have the largest coal areas.

(5) What is the difference between anthracite and bituminous coal? Name five of the states in which coal is found in large quantities.

United States History.—(1) Name a vice president of the United States who died before he could begin to perform the duties of his office.

(2) Name an American who was a poet, an essayist, and a diplomatist; one who was an essayist, a scientific investigator, and a statesman; two who were historians and diplomatists; one who was a poet and a diplomatist.

(3) Name three celebrated persons from each of the following-named states, and name one important event or work with which each person named was connected: Pennsylvania, Indiana, Massachusetts, Missouri, Virginia.

(4) Name the political parties which nominated the following-named candidates for President of the United States: James Birney, John Quincy Adams, Peter Cooper, Lewis Cass, Winfield Scott, John Parker Hale, Horace Greeley.

(5) Name a President of the United States who was censured by the senate; another who was censured by the house. State briefly the reasons for the action in each case.

General Information.—(1) Against what evils were the following-named books a protest: Nicholas

Nickleby, Don Quixote, Les Miserables, Little Dorrit, Uncle Tom's Cabin?

(2) What book or other literary work does each of the following names suggest to you: Dromio, Hopeful, Trinculo, Currer Bell, Wilhelm Meister, Thoreau, Cuttle, Motley, Jekyll, Gulliver?

(3) What are meant by the terms "chamber of commerce" and "board of trade"?

(4) What are cipher dispatches? Give an illustration of system.

(5) State briefly what you know concerning Alsace-Lorraine; its area, boundaries, language, government.

ANSWERS TO TEST QUESTIONS
No. 13.

Arithmetic.—(1) At midnight, 210 miles from Chicago and 280 miles from Kansas City.

(2) The cost of fencing the square would be to the cost of fencing the parallelogram as 1 : 1.45. Thus, supposing the cost to be 50 cents per rod, the expense of fencing the square would be $100, and that of the parallelogram, $145.

(3) The total area of the farm = 25,600 square rods. (a) Supposing the road to run along parallel sides:

Ravine's area $\quad = 60 \times 6 \quad = 360$ sq. rods.

Road's area $\quad = 160 \times 2 \times 2 = 640$ "

Timber land's area $= 40 \times 15 \quad = 600$ "

Area of untillable land $\quad = 1,600$ sq. rods.

25,600 sq. rods — 1,600 sq. rods = 24,000 sq. rods, or 150 acres.

(b) Supposing the road to run along adjacent sides, the amount of untillable land would be 4 sq. rods less, and the tillable land would be 25,600 sq. rods — 1,596 sq. rods = 24,004 sq. rods, or $150\frac{1}{40}$ acres.

(4) 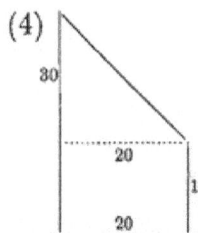 The upper 30 feet of the telephone pole would constitute the perpendicular of a right-angled triangle, of which the distance from the top of the post to the telephone pole (20 ft.) would be the base, and the wire the hypotenuse. $\sqrt{20^2 + 30^2} = \sqrt{1300} = 36.05+$ feet, length of the wire.

(5) The height of the pitch is $\frac{2}{3}$ of 24 feet $= 16$ feet, the distance from the vertex of the roof to the square. This is the altitude of a right-angled triangle whose base is half the width of the building (12 ft.), and whose hypotenuse is the length of the rafter. $\sqrt{16^2 + 12^2} = \sqrt{400} = 20$ feet, length of rafter.

———

Language and Grammar.—(1) It is my purpose to defeat his *nefarious* schemes. That man's dress is *incongruous*. There are several *discrepancies* in the statement made by the witness. He is a man of *ex-*

emplary character. *Precedent* is not a verb, but may be a noun or adjective; for example: "*Precedent* injury," "There is no *precedent* for this action." He treated his visitor with *contumely*. The *truculent* natives of Uganda. I will *contest* the election. There will be a *contest* between the two colleges.

(2) Realistic, fiction, finite, humble, nadir, torrid, fickle, atheist, praise, retrogression.

(3) *That* is a relative pronoun. *That* is the dog that bit me. *That* man is a good citizen. He will say *that* you may go.

(4) Any substantive, whether word, phrase, or clause.

(5) (*a*) I suppose he is sick. *Expect* means to look for, to look forward to, or to anticipate; hence is wrongly used in the sentence given. (*b*) They presented him a gold-headed cane. *With* is superfluous. (*c*) *Enthused* is slang. The sentence could be written in various ways, as: He aroused a great deal of enthusiasm in the meeting. (*d*) He died of a fever. The wrong preposition is used. (*c*) &c. is a disrespectful way of closing a letter, and is inexcusable.

———

Geography.—(1) Yes; at Chicago. About three inches.

(2) (*a*) Ice covering large surfaces. (*b*) A large, floating mass of ice. (*c*) Pieces of broken ice closely packed together. (*d*) Ice floating about.

(3) Lakes Huron and Ontario were at a remote period part of an arm of the sea. The Mohawk and Hudson valleys formed the rest of the arm.

(4) China, United States, Canada, India, Russia.

(5) (a) Anthracite coal is hard and compact, has a high luster, has but little bitumen; hence its flame is almost non-luminous. Bituminous coal contains much bitumen — a black, tarry substance — burns with a yellow, smoky flame, and is soft. (b) Pennsylvania, Missouri, Alabama, Illinois, Kansas.

United States History. — (1) William Rufus King. He was elected in 1852.

(2) (a) James Russell Lowell. (b) Benjamin Franklin. (c) John Lothrop Motley and George Bancroft. (d) Bayard Taylor.

(3) Pennsylvania: Benjamin Franklin, scientist and diplomat; author of "Poor Richard's Almanac." Stephen Girard, founder of Girard College. Albert Gallatin, financier, second secretary of the treasury of the United States. Indiana: Oliver P. Morton, statesman; great war governor during the rebellion. Lew Wallace, author of "The Fair God" and "Ben Hur." Benjamin Harrison, statesman, President of the United States. Massachusetts: Daniel Webster, statesman, most distinguished American orator; "Oration against Hayne." Horace Mann, greatest American educator; Massachusetts educational department. Nathaniel Hawthorne, greatest American

novelist; "Scarlet Letter." Missouri: Thomas H. Benton, statesman; wrote "Thirty Years in the United States Senate." James B. Eads, inventor and constructive engineer; built the great Mississippi river bridge at St. Louis, the jetties, etc. B. Gratz Brown, statesman; candidate on the liberal republican ticket for vice president, with Horace Greeley for President. Virginia: George Washington, general and statesman, commander of continental armies, and first President of the United States. James Madison, statesman, President of the United States during the war of 1812; author of a number of the *Federalist* papers. Thomas Jefferson, statesman, President of the United States; wrote declaration of independence and bought Louisiana.

(4) Liberty party; national republican; independpendent; democratic; whig; liberal republican.

(5) On March 28, 1834, the United States senate censured President Jackson for exercising powers not conferred upon him by the constitution when he removed the deposits from the United States Bank. In 1842, a report censuring President Tyler for vetoing a tariff bill was passed by the house of representatives.

General Information.—(1) (a) The brutalities which prevailed in private schools. (b) Knight-errantry. (c) The severity of French criminal law. (d) Debtors' prisons and "red tape" in government offices. (e) Slavery.

(2) (*a*) Comedy of Errors. (*b*) Pilgrim's Progress. (*c*) The Tempest. (*d*) Jane Eyre. (*e*) Book of that name, by Goethe. (*f*) Walden, or Life in the Woods. (*g*) Dombey and Son. (*h*) Rise of the Dutch Republic. (*i*) The Strange Case of Doctor Jekyll and Mr. Hyde. (*j*) Gulliver's Travels.

(3) They virtually mean the same thing. Chamber of commerce is defined by one authority to be "an assembly of merchants and traders where affairs relating to trade are treated of." Another authority gives this definition: "A society of the principal merchants and traders, who meet to promote the general commerce of the place."

(4) Dispatches written in signs made to correspond to letters of the alphabet, or by placing the letters out of their regular order. For instance, let the lower letter represent the upper, thus: a, b, c, d, l, m, n, o, e, f, g, h, i, j, k, l, m, n, o, p, q, r, s, t, u, v, x, y, z. p, q, r, s, t, u, v, x, y, z, a, b, c, d, e, f, g, h, i, j, k. Following this arrangement, if one wished to dispatch, "Hold the fort," the message would be as follows: "Saxo fsp qadf."

(5) Two provinces ceded by France to Germany at the close of the Franco German war in 1871. The territory is situated between France and Germany, has an area of 5,580 square miles. German is the prevailing language, but French is spoken by a considerable number of the people. Much of the French population left for France when the provinces were surrendered to Germany.

PRONOUNCING CONTEST—No. 13.

Projectile, redolent, exigency, eyrie, corps diplomatique, derisive, Hebrides, irrefutable, peremptorily, Psyche, St. Augustine (city), St. Augustine (church father), simultaniety, sojourn (verb), sojourn (noun), tatterdemalion, Disraeli, learned (adjective).

TEST QUESTIONS—No. 14.

Arithmetic.—(1) How many square yards of clot!. will be required for a tent in the form of a cone 15 feet in diameter and 18 feet high?

(2) How many minutes were there from 10:40 A. M., February 4, 1892, to 1:30 P. M., March 2, 1892?

(3) The assessed valuation of a certain school district is $9,000. It is allowed by law to levy a tax of 2 mills on each dollar of valuation. The district receives $25 a year from the state school fund. Coal and other incidental expenses amount to $40 a year. How much, if the full rate is levied, will be left for teachers' wages? If the average teacher is worth $40 a month, and the length of the school term should be nine months, how much does the district lack?

(4) The area of the grounds of a schoolhouse is one acre. The schoolhouse is 24 feet long, and 16 feet wide. What percentage of the grounds does the schoolhouse occupy?

(5) What percentage in grains is a pound troy of a pound avoirdupois? An ounce troy of an ounce avoirdupois? What percentage in cubic inches is a pint, liquid measure, of a peck, dry measure?

Language and Grammar.—(1) Make sentences in which the following words are used correctly: Emigration, immigration, nepotism, persuasive, peremptory, predilection, surveillance, suavity, illusive, elusive.

(2) Write the participles of the following verbs: Fight, sit, set.

(3) What is meant by a double relative? Give example of its use.

(4) Give the plural form for molasses, mouse, fish, memorandum, politics.

(5) "It rains." "It is he." Why are the foregoing expressions correct? What grammatical rules do they seem to violate? What name is given to such expressions?

Geography.—(1) Where is Two Ocean pass, and why so named?

(2) What is meant by "The Roaring Forties"?

(3) Substitute the right name for each of the following: Far Cathay, The Floating City, The Eye of the East, The Queen of the Antilles, Land of the Rising Sun.

(4) Name the largest peninsula in the world, tell where it is situated, and give approximately its area.

(5) Name the largest inland sheet of water in the world, tell where it is situated, and what may be remarkable about it, and give approximately its area.

United States History.—(1) A graduate of Harvard was a delegate to the Continental Congress, 1784–'86; was United States senator; then minister to Great Britain; again United States senator; and, again, minister to Great Britain. Name him.

(2) A graduate of Princeton was in succession United States senator, minister to Russia, vice president of the United States, minister to Great Britain. Name him.

(3) Give the number of senators and representatives in the Congress of 1790, and the ratio of representation. Give the number and ratio in 1893.

(4) After a state is admitted into the Union, when does its star appear on our national flag?

(5) Beginning with 1800, give the percentage of increase in population in the United States every 10 years, to and including 1890.

General Information.—(1) What is meant by each of the following words: Autonomy, armistice, oligarchy, bureaucracy?

(2) What is "filibustering" in parliamentary law?

(3) Define "funding" and "refunding."

(4) Name the countries in Europe which have two legislative chambers, which have but one, and which have no legislature.

(5) How many times and in what manner has the government of France been changed since 1789?

ANSWERS TO TEST QUESTIONS
No. 14.

Arithmetic.—(1) Slant height $= \sqrt{18^2 + 7\frac{1}{2}^2} =$ 19.5. Half slant height $= 9.75$ ft. Circumference of base $= 15 \times 3.1416 = 47.124$ ft. $47.124 \times 9.75 = 459.459$ sq. ft. $= 51.051$ yards.

(2) From 10:40 A. M. to midnight, February 4, $1892 = 13\frac{1}{3}$ hours. From February 4 to 1:30 P. M., March 2, $1892 = 26$ days, $13\frac{1}{2}$ hours. Total number of hours from 10:40 A. M., February 4, to 1:30 P. M., March 2, $650\frac{1}{2}$; total number of minutes, 39,050.

(3) We should have have written 20 mills instead of 2.

$$\$9,000 \times .020 = \$180.$$
$$180 + \$25 = 205.$$
$$205 - 40 = 165.$$
$$165 \div 40 = 4\frac{1}{8}.$$

The district lacks $4\frac{7}{8}$ months of school, even though the maximum rate of taxation is levied.

(4) 1 A. $= 43,560$ sq ft. Area occupied by schoolhouse $= 384$ sq. ft. Percentage of the grounds occupied by the schoolhouse, $.0088+$.

(5) (a) $82\frac{2}{7}$. (b) $109+$. (c) $5.37+$.

Language and Grammar.—(1) There will be a heavy *emigration* of negroes from the Southern states to Liberia. It is hoped that the *immigration* to Kansas this year will be very great. In his appointments the comptroller can justly be charged with *nepotism*. The *persuasive* powers of that lawyer are very great. In a *peremptory* manner he told him to leave the room. The judge had a *predilection* for the prisoner. The police had him under *surveillance* while he remained in the city. He was a man of much *suavity* of manners. Life is *illusive.* He answered me in an *elusive* manner.

(2) Fight: fighting, fought, having fought, being fought, having been fought. Sit: sitting, sat, having sat. Set: setting, set, having set. Being set, having been set.

(3) The double relative is the pronoun "what." It is so called because it may be separated into "that which." Example: He will do what is right.

(4) (*a*) Has no plural form. (*b*) Mice. (*c*) Fish or fishes. (*d*) Memoranda or memorandums. (*e*) Has no plural form.

(5) (*a*) Because the immemorial usage of the best English writers and speakers has sanctioned those forms. (*b*) "It" is singular, and is used to represent the plural noun "elements." "It" is neuter, and is the antecedent of "he" which is masculine. (*c*) They are called idioms.

Geography.—(1) In the Yellowstone region. So named because the waters flow in opposite directions —part toward the Atlantic; part toward the Pacific.

(2) Below 40 deg. south latitude the anti-trade winds blow more steadily than elsewhere.   These winds have been named "The Roaring Forties" by seamen.

(3) China, Bangkok, Damascus, Cuba, Japan.

(4) Arabia.   Western Asia.   More than one million square miles.

(5) Caspian sea.   Southeastern Russia, between Europe and Asia.   Its waters are salt.   170,000 square miles.

United States History.—(1) Rufus King.

(2) George Mifflin Dallas.

(3) In 1790, number of representatives, 65; ratio of representatives, 30,000.   In 1893, number, 356; ratio, 173,901.

(4) On the 4th of July following the admission of the state.

(5) 1800, 35+ per cent.; 1810, 36+; 1820, 33+; 1830, 33+; 1840, 32+; 1850, 35.8+; 1860, 35.5+; 1870, 22.6+; 1880, 30+; 1890, 24.8+.

General Information.—(1) (a) It originally meant the power of self-government, but the word now is understood to mean the independence in local matters which a state itself, part of a confederation, may have, subject to the national constitution or laws. Thus, the states of the American union, of the German empire and the cantons of Switzerland have autonomy. (*b*) A temporary suspension of hostilities between two armies by mutual agreement. (*c*) Government in which the power is placed in the hands of a few persons. (*d*) The exercise of undue influence and authority by the collective bureaus of a government.

(2) The tactics by which a minority in a legislative body obstructs obnoxious legislation. These tactics may be in numerous forms, such as making motions to adjourn, rising to points of order, moving to lay on the table, moving to reconsider, long speeches, etc.

(3) (*a*) To convert a floating debt into interest-bearing bonds. (*b*) The renewal of a debt which has been already funded.

(4) (*a*) Great Britain, France, Spain, Italy, Austria, Germany, Switzerland, Denmark, Holland, Belgium, Sweden, and Norway. (*b*) Greece, Servia, and Bulgaria. (*c*) Russia and Turkey.

(5) Twelve times. Republic 1793, directory (government by five directors), consulate (government by three consuls), consulate (first consul given extraordinary powers), the first empire, the monarchy, first empire restored, monarchy restored, monarchy by election, republic, the second empire, the republic.

PRONOUNCING CONTEST— No. 14.

Molecule, molecular, sedative, pathos, glacial, dromedary, brigantine, roseola, decorous, pyrites, misconstrue, hypochondriac, coterie, academian, grease (noun), grease (verb), hospitable, occult, probatory, remediless.

TEST QUESTIONS—No. 15.

Arithmetic.—(1) My watch gains 55 seconds per day. I put it right at 4 P. M. on Saturday. What time will it be by my watch at 10 A. M. on the following Thursday?

(2) I sold the N. E. ¼ of the S. E. ¼ of the N. W. ¼ of a section of land at $12.75 an acre. How much did I get for the land?

(3) If I go diagonally across from the S. E. corner to the N. W. corner of the S. W. ¼ of the S.W. ¼ of a section of land instead of going on the boundary lines, how much do I save in the distance?

(4) How many barrels (31½ gallons) will a cubical cistern that is 8 feet deep contain?

(5) How many hours will there be in the year 1900?

Language and Grammar.—(1) Make sentences in which the following words are used correctly : Coterie, naïve, nave, façade, portentous, ominous, accession, tension, retentive, promulgate.

(2) Correct the following, and give reasons for each correction: "He took up school." "I do not blame the failure on Jones." "There is no doubt but what he will go."

(3) Define euphemism, euphony, repartee, and give an example of each.

(4) What is meant by poetical license? Illustrate.

(5) What is blank verse? Give an example.

Geography.—(1) Give the meaning of low barometer and high barometer.

(2) Why is it that the water of the ocean does not freeze as readily as fresh water? Is there any difference in composition between the ice on the ocean and the water from which it is formed?

(3) Name an island on which a celebrated author died; another on which a noted general died; one on which a great general was born; and two which are named in a popular hymn.

(4) What is meant by each of the following words: Boers, Maoris, Papuans, atoll, mosque?

(5) What and where are pusstas, salvas, steppes, llanos, pampas?

United States History.—(1) A certain man was successively pastor of a church, representative in Congress, governor of a state, minister to Great Britain, secretary of state, United States senator, candidate for vice president. Name him and his native state.

(2) What is meant by the term "pocket veto"?

(3) What was the "Ostend Manifesto"? and by whom was it issued?

(4) When was a blockade of the Southern ports proclaimed? When and by whom was the blockade raised?

(5) How much was the debt of the United States in 1860? How much in 1865?

General Information.—(1) What is the origin of the term "grain," used in troy and avoirdupois weights?

(2) Give the origin of each of the following words: Augury, sophistry, auspices, mortgage, blackmail.

(3) Name the author of each of the following quotations:

"Who does the best his circumstance allows,
   Does well, acts nobly; angels could do no more."
"For just experience tells in every soil
   That those who think must govern those who toil."
"I am a part of all that I have met."
"Measure your mind's height by the shade it casts."

(4) Whence were the names of the seven days of the week derived?

(5) In a few words, tell what you know about the "long" parliament.

ANSWERS TO TEST QUESTIONS
No. 15.

Arithmetic.—(1) The time from 4 P. M. on Saturday to 10 A. M. on the following Thursday $= 4\frac{3}{4}$ days 55 sec. $\times 4\frac{3}{4} = 261\frac{1}{4}$ sec. $= 4$ min. 17 sec. Hence, the time will be 4 min. 17 sec. after 10 A. M. on Thursday.

(2) The N. E. $\frac{1}{4}$ of the S. E. $\frac{1}{4}$ of the N. W. $\frac{1}{4}$ of a section of land (not fractional) $= 10$ acres. $12.75 $\times 10 = $127.50.

(3) If I go on the boundary lines, I must travel 320 rods   The diagonal $= \sqrt{160^2 + 160^2} = 226.45+$. $320 - 226.45+ = 93.55$. Hence, I save 93.55 rods in distance.

(4) $8^3 \times 1728 = 884736 =$ number of cubic inches in cistern. $\frac{884736}{231} = 3830+ =$ number of gals. in the cistern. $3830+ \div 31\frac{1}{2} = 12+ =$ number of barrels.

(5) The year 1900 is the last in the century. It is not a leap year because its number is not divisible by 400. Hence, the number of hours $= 24$ hrs. $\times 365 = 8,760$ hrs.

Language and Grammar.—(1) The brilliant *coteries* of Boston. She told her story in a *naive* manner. There is a *nave* in the cathedral. That building has a beautiful *façade*. These dark clouds in the west are *portentous*. His frown is *ominous*. The *accession* of Alaska to the United States was of great importance. The *tension* on his muscles was very painful. He has a *retentive* memory. He is about to *promulgate* a decree.

(2) (*a*) He *began* the school. Because the other expression is slang. (*b*) I do not blame Jones *for* the failure. You cannot blame a failure *on* anybody. The entire expression is an ungrammatical jumble. (*c*) There is no doubt but h will go. *What* is superfluous.

(3) (*a*) A figure by which a mild or inoffensive word is substituted for a harsh one. Example: He *abstracted* (stole) a handkerchief from the counter. (*b*) An easy and a smooth enunciation of sounds. Example: "The wolf's long howl on Onalooska's shore." (*c*) A smart, ready and witty reply. Example: "What's going on?" said a bore who stopped Douglas Jerrold on the street. "I am," replied Jerrold, passing on.

(4) Poets sometimes violate the rules of syntax, and this practice is called "poetical license." Example: "And in the lowest deep a lower deep." "Where echo walks steep hills among."

(5) Measures in poetry in which there are no rhymes, usually each verse ends with an important word. Example:

> "From morn
> To noon he fell, from noon to dewy eve,
> A summer's day; and with the setting sun
> Dropped from the zenith like a falling star.'
> — *Milton.*

Geography.—(1) When the air is heavy it pushes the mercury in a barometer up; when the air is light, the mercury falls.

(2) Because the freezing of salt water takes place at a lower temperature than that of fresh water. Salt water freezes at 29 deg. Fah., fresh at 32 deg. Fah.

(3) Robert Louis Stevenson died on Upolu, one of the Samoan islands. Napoleon died on the island of St. Helena, and he was born on the island of Corsica. Greenland and Ceylon are named in the hymn "From Greenland's Icy Mountains."

(4) (*a*) The inhabitants of two republics, the Orange River Free State, and the South African Republic, both in South Africa. (*b*) The original natives of New Zealand. (*c*) The natives of the Australasian islands. (*d*) Islands ring-shaped, and wholly composed of the skeletons of *coral polyps*, situated in the Pacific ocean. (*e*) A Mohammedan church.

(5) (*a*) Great plains of Hungary. (*b*) *Selvas* (misprinted *salvas*) are the great forests of the Amazon valley. (*c*) The great treeless plains of Russia. Also applied to the plains of Patagonia. (*d*) The plains of the lower Orinoco. (*e*) The treeless plains of the Argentine Republic.

United States History.—(1) Edward Everett.

(2) Bills passed during the last ten days of a

session, if kept by the President until Congress adjourns, do not become laws. Hence, this way of nullifying a bill is called "pocket veto."

(3) On October 9, 1854, James Buchanan, John Y. Mason, and Pierre Soulé, the American ministers to Great Britain, France, and Spain, met at Ostend, under the direction of President Pierce, and drew up the dispatch to the United States government, now known as the "Ostend Manifesto." The substance of this dispatch was that the sale of Cuba would be as advantageous and honorable to Spain as its purchase would be to the United States, but that if Spain refused to sell it, self-preservation would make it necessary for the United States to wrest it from her.

(4) (*a*) On April 23, 1861, by President Lincoln. (*b*) On May 22, 1865, by President Johnson. The blockade in Texas was not raised until a month later.

(5) (*a*) $64,842,287. (*b*) $2,680,647,869.

General Information.—(1) The old English pound was equal to the weight of 7,680 grains of wheat, hence, the name grain. The standard has changed since that time.

(2) (*a*) The augurs in ancient Rome were a college or board whose duty it was to interpret the signs of approval or disapproval which Jupiter was supposed to send in regard to any public transaction. Hence, our word *augury*. (*b*) Derived from a school of

philosophy in ancient Greece, the members of which
were known as sophists. They were noted for their
ingenuity in making the worse appear the better reason. Hence, our word *sophistry*, meaning a reasoning
which is sound in appearance only. (*d*) Synonym
of auguries. (*e*) From two French words, *mort*
dead, and *gage*, a pledge, so called because in case of
nonpayment of the debt, the land was forever *dead*,
and lost to the mortgagor. (*d*) A certain rate of
money, corn or cattle paid to bands of robbers in the
south of Scotland and north of England, which
secured to those who paid the protection of the robbers.

(3) (*a*) Rogers. (*b*) Goldsmith. (*c*) Tennyson.
(*d*) Browning.

(4) From the names of Pagan gods. Sunday,
Sun's day; Monday, Moon's day; Tuesday, Tuisto
or Tuesco (Saxon god); Wednesday, Woden's day;
Thursday, Thor's day; Friday, Friga (Scandinavian
god); Saturday, Saterne's day.

(5) It met in November, 1640. It attainted the
Earl of Stratford; abolished the star chamber; the
raising of tonnage and poundage without the consent
of parliament was declared illegal, and it was provided that parliament could not be dissolved without
its own consent. This parliament began and carried
on the contest which culminated in the execution of
Charles I, and the establishment of the common-
wealth. The long parliament was dissolved by
Cromwell in 1653.

PRONOUNCING CONTEST—No. 15.

Parasitism, mechanist, metamorphism, misconstrue, occultism, odometer, panegyrize, pantomimist, periphrasis, predicamental, prelatism, severable, sequestration, secretory, above, giaour, oaths, beneath, eider, Nassau.

TEST QUESTIONS — No. 16.

Arithmetic.—(1) Reduce 14 bushels 3 pecks to pints, and analyze in three ways.

(2) A surveyor stands at the point A. The first chain man stands due west of A 45 rods; the second chain man stands 60 rods due north of the first. What is the shortest distance from the surveyor to the second chain man?

(3) How many minutes will there be in the year 2000?

(4) Subtract $\frac{7}{8}$ of a leap year from a common year, and give the difference in hours, minutes, and seconds.

(5) The assessed valuation of A's farm and personal property is $900. He pays 2 per cent. school tax; 4 mills on the dollar township tax; 3 mills county tax; 2 mills state tax. Give the amount of his taxes.

Language and Grammar.—(1) Make sentences in which the following words are used correctly: Impervious, homogeneous, imperturbable, incisive, poignant, mediocre, erudite, episode, epitome, equivocal.

(2) Name five adjectives that cannot be compared.

(3) Correct the following, and give reasons for

each correction: "I am stopping at the hotel;" "In so far as that may be true;" "All of my classmates are going to the picnic."

(4) Define tautology and pleonasm, and give an example of each.

(5) Define verse, distich or couplet, and triplet, and give an example of each.

Geography.—(1) How does the captain of a ship ascertain in what longitude and latitude his ship is at any time?

(2) Give approximately the number of people belonging to each of the five races of mankind.

(3) Tell briefly what is the work of the United States weather bureau.

(4) Why is it that the western part of the Argentine Republic has but little moisture, while nearly all the western part of Brazil has a great deal?

(5) Name the most important of the colonies or protectorates of France.

United States History.—(1) What is the origin of the term "corporal's guard" in United States history?

(2) He was a lawyer, governor of his state, minister to Great Britain, minister to Spain, candidate for President, member of congress, major general during a great war. Name him.

(3) What was the "Salary Grab"?

(4) What is meant by "subsidies"? Give illus-
trations.

(5) Name three states which were formed from
parts of states already in existence.

———

General Information. — (1) Whence were the
names of the months derived?

(2) What is the difference between a privateer
and a pirate?

(3) Name the author of each of the following
quotations: "Well said; that was laid on with a
trowel." "He makes no friend who never made a
foe." "For he who is honest is noble, whatever his
fortunes or birth."

(4) What changes have taken place in the government of Spain since 1800?

(5) Tell what you can concerning Corea and its
people in 100 words?

ANSWERS TO TEST QUESTIONS
No. 16.

Arithmetic.— (1)

(a)
$$\begin{array}{c} \text{Bu.} \quad \text{Pks.} \\ 14 - 3 \\ 4 \\ \hline 59 \\ 8 \\ \hline 472 \\ 2 \\ \hline 944 \text{ pints.} \end{array}$$

(b) 14.75 bu. $\times 4 \times 8 \times 2 = 944$ pts.

(c) $14\frac{3}{4}$ bu. $\times 4 \times 8 \times 2 = 944$ pts.

NOTE—The analysis is simply indicated. The pupil can expand it.

(2) The distance from the surveyor $= \sqrt{40^2 + 60^2}$ $= 78.7 +$ rods.

(3) In the year 2,000 there will be 366 days. 366 days $\times 24 \times 60 = 527,040$ minutes.

(4) 366 days $\times 24 = 8,784$ hours = number of hours in a leap year. 8,784 of $\frac{7}{8} = 7,686$ hours. $8,760 - 7,686 = 1,074$ hours.

(5)

$900 \times .02 \ = \$18.00 =$ school tax.
$900 \times .004 = 3.60 =$ township tax.
$900 \times .003 = 2.70 =$ county tax.
$900 \times .002 = 1.80 =$ state tax.

Total, $\$26.10$.

Language and Grammar.— (1) He is *impervious* to ridicule. The French are a *homogeneous* people. Under this torrent of abuse, he remained as *imper-*

turbable as a graven image. In an *incisive* speech he exposed the weakness of the party's policy. The loss of his brother caused him *poignant* sorrow. He is a man of *mediocre* abilities. He was a most *erudite* teacher. This was the most interesting *episode* in the narrative. We have in these few paragraphs an *epitome* of the entire work. He gave me an *equivocal* answer.

(2) Circular, square, wooden, two, daily.

(3) (*a*) I am *staying* at the hotel. Because stop is the reverse of start, and is incorrectly used. (*b*) So far as that may be true. *In* is superfluous. (*c*) All my classmates are going to the picnic. *Of* is unnecessary, and adds nothing to clearness of expression.

(4) (*a*) It is a needless repetition of an idea in different words and phrases. Example: "Said party of the first part doth *covenant* and *agree*." (*b*) The use of more words than are necessary to express an idea. Example: "He returned *back again* to his native state."

(5) (*a*) A single line of poetry. Example:

"Life is real, life is earnest."

(*b*) A couple of lines making complete sense. Example:

"Know thyself, presume not God to scan;
The proper study of mankind is man."

(*c*) Three lines rhyming together. Example:

"As she fled fast through sun and shade,
The happy winds upon her played,
Blowing the ringlets from the braid."

Geography.—(1) (*a*) By comparing the time at Greenwich on the prime meridian with the noon instant where the ship is at that time, the longitude is computed. Every ship has a chronometer set to the time on the prime meridian. An allowance of 15 degrees is made for each hour. (*b*) The latitude is determined by measuring with a sextant the angle made by the sun with the horizon at noon.

(2) Caucasian, about 600,000,000. Mongolian, about 600,000,000. Ethiopian, about 180,000,000. Malay, between 50,000,000 and 60,000,000. Indian, about 10,000,000.

(3) To make observations and records relating to the weather. Observation stations are maintained by the government in different parts of the United States. From these the condition of the temperature, appearance of the sky, pressure of the atmosphere, rain or snowfall, are telegraphed to Washington twice a day from the several observation points. From the bureau at Washington predictions concerning the weather, based upon the reports received, are sent by telegraph to central points in all parts of the country.

(4) (*a*) In the temperate zone, in which zone the Argentine Republic is situated, the moisture is carried from the Pacific, but is condensed by the cold, western summits and slopes of the Andes, and flows back into the Pacific. Hence, the western part of the Argentine Republic, being east of the Andes, receives but little moisture. (*b*) In the torrid zone,

the moisture is carried westward by the trade winds blowing from the Atlantic. The moisture is condensed on the eastern summits and slopes of the Andes; hence, western Brazil has a great deal of rain.

(5) Algeria, Tunis, New Caledonia, Anam, Madagascar.

United States History.—(1) A name given in derision to the few who supported President Tyler's policy from 1841 to 1845.

(2) Thomas Pinckney, South Carolina.

(3) The name given by the people to the act passed by Congress in 1873, increasing federal salaries. The President's salary was increased from $25,000 to $50,000; of the chief justice, from $8,500 to $10,-000; of the associate justices, cabinet officers, vice president, and speaker of the house, from $8,000 to $10,000; of senators and representatives, from $5,000 to $7,500. What gave rise to the term "salary grab" was, that the act was made retroactive, and that the members of the Congress which passed the law were to receive the increase in salary from the beginning of their respective terms. In January, 1874, the act, except that part of it relating to the President and justices, was repealed.

(4) Generally speaking, it means aid, in money, granted by the state to persons engaged in enterprises of a mercantile, manufacturing or industrial character. Specifically, it means money paid by a government to

steamboat or railroad companies. The United States government has paid subsidies to lines from New York to Liverpool, Panama to Oregon, Charleston to Havana, and New York to Brazil.

(5) West Virginia, Kentucky, and Maine.

———

General Information.—(1) From the Romans. January, *Januaris*, from *Janus;* February, *Februaris*, from *Februa;* March, *Martius*, from Mars; April, *Aprilis*, from *Aperio;* May, *Maius*, from *Maia;* June, *Junius*, from *Juno;* July, *Julius*, from Julius Cæsar; August, *Augustus*, from Augustus Cæsar; September means seventh month; October, eighth month; November, ninth month; December, tenth month. Originally, the Roman year began with March, and the number of months was 10.

(2) (*a*) A pirate is a ship which carries on robbery by force on the sea. (*b*) A privateer is an armed ship, owned by one or more private persons, to whom in time of war a government grants a commission authorizing the owner or owners and crew to capture the enemy's ships or other property, and to appropriate to themselves, in whole or in part, the ships and goods seized.

(3) Shakespeare; Tennyson; Alice Cary.

(4) In 1808, Napoleon drove out the reigning monarch and placed his own brother, Joseph Bonaparte, on the throne. In 1814, Frederick VII, the former monarch, was restored. In 1868, Queen

Is abella was driven out of the country, and, in 1870 Amadeus Hosta, second son of Victor Emanuel, accepted the crown, but he resigned a few years later. A republic was formed, and that gave place to the monarchy in 1874, when the crown was offered to Alfonso, son of the exiled queen. During the period from 1800 until the present (1895), there have been many rebellions in Spain; but few of them led to radical changes.

(5) Corea is a kingdom of eastern Asia, occupying a peninsula bounded on the east by the Sea of Japan on the west by the Yellow sea; south, by the Strait of Corea; north, by Manchuria. Corea is a mountainous country, and is said to be rich in minerals. The temperature is more even than that of the Asiatic continent, but in the northern part it is very cold. The king has been a vassal of China, but within the limits of Corea his power has been absolute. The late war between Japan and China has made Corea an independent state.

PRONOUNCING CONTEST—No. 16.

Redolent, patois, pæony, mitrailleuse, contemporaneity, jurisconsult, placable, proscenium, varioloid, contemplator, isochronal, sepulture, lichens, cotyledon, clinique, improvvisatore, anabasis, Tehuantepec, Sanhedrin, Saguenay.

TEST QUESTIONS — No. 17.

Arithmetic.— (1) What must be the length of each side of a cubical granary which is to hold 1,000 bushels of wheat?

(2) The length of the school term in a certain school district was 6 months of 20 days each. One of the pupils was absent during the term 16 days, and he was tardy 15 minutes every day he was present. How much of the term did he lose?

(3) The scale on a map is 8 miles to the inch. How many square miles are there in a county which is represented on the map by a rectangle $4\frac{1}{2}$ inches long and $2\frac{3}{4}$ inches wide? How many acres are there in the county?

(4) The fare on Kansas railroads is 3 cents a mile. Persons purchasing return tickets receive a discount of 10 per cent. If a return ticket costs me $7.56, what is the distance between the two stations?

(5) What percentage of the area of Kansas are the combined areas of Maine, Vermont, New Hampshire, Massachusetts, Connecticut, Rhode Island, and New Jersey? (See any modern geography for areas.)

Language and Grammar.— (1) Make sentences in which the following words are used correctly: Excruciating, facile, versatile, exuberant, docile, inimical, irrefragable, metamorphosed, moribund.

(2) Write the plural and the possessive singular of each of the following words: Court-martial, man-trap, cousin-german. Give the rules which are followed.

(3) Correct the following, and give reasons for each correction: "That book will do equally as well." "Had I have gone to school yesterday, I should have been first in my class." "I intend to pay my arrearages soon."

(4) What is meant by "obscurity" in rhetoric? Give an example.

(5) What is alliteration? Give examples.

Geography.—(1) Where are the loftiest plateaus in the world?

(2) Where is the most foggy place in the world? Why is it so foggy there?

(3) What are *moraines* and *crevasses?*

(4) Explain the flag signals of the United States weather bureau.

(5) A certain country exports sugar, cotton, wool. Its capital is seven miles from the sea. The eastern part of the country is fertile; the western, arid. The form of government is republican. Name the country.

United States History.—(1) What is meant by the "Amistad case"?

(2) What is the "Order of the Cincinnati"?

(3) When did the Hartford convention meet? What were its purposes?

(4) Who were the "Coodies"?

(5) What was the "Covode investigation"?

General Information.—(1) What countries were represented at the Paris monetary conference of 1867?

(2) What is meant by the "previous question" in parliamentary law?

(3) Name the author of each of the following quotations: "Heaven is above all yet; there sits a judge that no king can corrupt." "A man of pleasure is a man of pains." "Truth is truth howe'er it strike."

(4) In what year was there a month which had but 19 days, and which had no new moon? Why?

(5) Give the origin of the words *clue, clumsy, coast, forestall, heathens.*

ANSWERS TO TEST QUESTIONS

No. 17.

Arithmetic.—(1) A bushel contains 1.25 cubic feet, nearly; 1,000 bushels contain 1,250 cubic feet, nearly. The cube root of $1,250 = 10.82$ feet, nearly, length of each side of required granary.

(2) $20 \times 6 = 120$ days. $120 - 16 = 104$ days. $15 \times 104 = 1,560$ minutes $= 26$ hours $= 4\frac{1}{3}$ school days. Total number of days lost, $108\frac{1}{3}$.

(3) $8 \times 4.5 \;\;= \;\; 36$ miles $=$ length.
  $8 \times 2.75 = \;\; 22$ miles $=$ breadth.
  $36 \times 26 \;\;\; = 640 = 599,040$ acres.

(4) $\$7.56 = 90\%$ of total fare; $7.56 \div 90 = .084$, or 1% of total fare; $.084 \times 100 = \$8.40$, or total fare; $840 \div 3 = 280$ miles.

(5) Area of Kansas, 82,080 square miles. Combined area of Maine, Vermont, New Hampshire, Massachusetts, Connecticut, Rhode Island, and New Jersey, 73,030 square miles, The percentage is $88+$.

———

Language and Grammar.—(1) The pain he suffered was *excruciating*. He is a *facile* writer. He was a *versatile* politician. The foliage was *exuberant*. That is a *docile* child. The course he is pursuing is *inimical* to your interests. He proved his case by *irrefragable* testimony. That man seems to have been *metamorphosed*. The patient is *moribund*.

(2) Courts-martial, man-traps, cousins-german. In compound words, the part which describes the rest is generally the part pluralized. When a compound word is composed of a noun and an adjective, the sign of the plural should be added to the noun.

(3) That book will do equally well. *As* is superfluous. Had I gone to school yesterday, I should have been first in my class. *Have* is unnecessary, and adds nothing to the clearness of the expression. The third sentence appears to be grammatically correct, but in other respects it seems to be wrong; at any rate, the arrearages have not come.

(4) A confusion in the expression of thought, usually because the thought itself is confused. Example: "The serene aspect of these writers, joined with the great encouragement I observe is given to another, or what is intended to be suspected, in which he indulges himself, confirmed me in the notion I have of the prevalence of ambition this way."

(5) The repetition of the same letter at the beginning of two or more words succeeding each other, or at short intervals. The recurrence of the same word in accented parts of words is also called alliteration. Example:

Fly o'er waste *fens* and windy *fields.—Tennyson.*
—International Dictionary.

Geography.—(1) In Thibet. They are from 10,000 to 15,000 feet high.

(2) On the Banks of Newfoundland. The vapor arising from the warm waters of the Gulf stream meets on the banks the cold current from the north. The vapor is condensed into fog continually.

(3) (*a*) The rocks and *debris* brought down by avalanches to the edge of glaciers, and which form a dark band on each side. (*b*) Fissures in glaciers.

(4) White flag, clear or fair weather; blue flag, general rain or snow; half-white and half-blue flag, local rain or snow; white flag with a black square in the center, a cold wave; black triangular flag, change in temperature; temperature flag above fair-weather or rain flag, warmer weather; below them, colder weather; no temperature flag means continuation of present temperature.

(5) Peru.

_____

United States History.—(1) On June 27, 1839, the *L'Amistad* was on her way from Havana to Puerto Principe with a cargo of slaves. The slaves mutinied, and killed all the crew except two, who were saved to navigate the ship to Africa. They, however, steered her in the direction of New York. She was seized by a United States warship — *Calderon.* The Spanish minister demanded the surrender of the slaves, on the ground that they were "property rescued from pirates." The abolitionists took the side of the slaves, and finally the supreme court decided that the slaves should be set free.

(2) It was founded by the officers of the revolutionary war, when the army was disbanded. Membership was limited to officers. The order is still in existence.

(3) A convention of leading representatives of the federalists opposed to the war of 1812. It was composed of 27 members. Massachusetts, Connecticut, New Hampshire, Vermont and Rhode Island were represented. Resolutions recommending that the South be deprived of the representation given it for three-fifths of its slaves, that a two-thirds vote be required to admit a territory, that naturalized foreigners be debarred from holding offices or sitting in Congress, were passed.

(4) A section of the federalists in New York city, in 1812, in favor of the war with England. The name was derived from the *nom de plume*—Abimalech Coody — of the leader, Gulian C. Verplanck.

(5) In the first session of the thirty-sixth congress, a committee, headed by Covode, of Pennsylvania, was appointed by the house of representatives to investigate charges of corruption made by two anti-Lecompton members against President Buchanan. The majority report was against the President.

General Information.—(1) Austria, Baden, Bavaria, Belgium, Denmark, the United States, France, Great Britain, Greece, Italy, The Netherlands, Portugal, Prussia, Russia, Sweden and Norway, Switzerland, Turkey, and Wurtumberg.

(2) It is the name for a motion that debate cease at once, and that a vote be taken on the question under discussion.

(3) Shakespeare, Young, Robert Browning.

(4) In 1752, the month of September had but 19 days, and had no new moon. The change from the old to the new style of dating had been made a short time before.

(5) (*a*) From the custom of unwinding a ball or *clew* of thread when one went through a labyrinth, in order to find the way back. (*b*) In old English, *clomsid* meant hands frozen or stiffened, hence unable to grasp anything. (*c*) From the Latin *costa*, a rib or side. (*d*) From the custom of certain buyers, who would buy of the dealer while he was on his way to his *stall* in market. (*e*) "The word *heathen* acquired its meaning from the fact that, at the introduction of Christianity into Germany, the wild dwellers on the *heaths* longest resisted the truth."—*Trench.*

PRONOUNCING CONTEST — No. 17.

Absolute, resolute, constitute, institute, blue, dew, due, blew, does, said, been, Kansas, Topeka, Iowa, Massachusetts, induce, hand, aunt, calm, ant.

TEST QUESTIONS — No. 18.

Arithmetic.—(1) If a 124 ft. steeple casts a 93 ft. shadow, what is the height of a steeple that casts a 162 ft. shadow, under the same conditions?

(2) Amount sent $2,530; commission, $2\frac{1}{2}$ per cent.; find amount paid out.

(3) Reduce 1 gi. to the decimal of a gallon.

(4) 5 seconds is what part of a degree?

(5) When it is noon in Boston (71° 3′ 30″ W.), what time is it at San Francisco (122° 26′ 15″ W.)?

Language and Grammar.—(1) What degree of comparison is expressed by each of the following: Better, ill, least, more? Write the three forms for each.

(2) What is an idiomatic phrase? Give three examples.

(3) Correct such of the following as are incorrect, and give reasons for so doing: (*a*) Will we ever be satisfied? (*b*) Should they be satisfied? (*c*) Would we be satisfied should we go? (*d*) You should be satisfied. (*e*) If I should be satisfied, would you be contented?

(4) Write the past tense for the following verbs: Beware, may, must, shall, ought.

(5) Correct the following: (*a*) He did not pay over $4 for the hat. (*b*) He is a man of considerable talent. (*c*) Here are a couple of apples. (*d*) He graduated from the Kansas university yesterday. (*e*) Will you jeopardize your fortunes?

Geography.—(1) What country in the world leads in the production of iron, of steel, of coal?

(2) Name in their order the five greatest wheat-producing countries of the earth.

(3) Name the three countries of the earth which have more than a half thousand inhabitants to each square mile of territory.

(4) Name the four countries (not governments) of the earth which support more than 50,000,000 people each.

(5) Name the three countries of the earth which have an area of more than 3,000,000 square miles.

United States History.— (1) What was the "kitchen cabinet"?

(2) What was the cause and what the result of the "Modoc war"?

(3) What was the greatest Christmas gift ever received by a President of the United States while in office?

(4) What was the pan-American congress?

(5) What peculiar coincidences occurred in con-

nection with the Washington and Bunker Hill monuments?

_____

General Information.—(1) What is meant by the phrase "tariff for revenue only," which occurs in United States political history?

(2) What schoolmaster in the time of Queen Elizabeth apologized for writing his books in English?

(3) What is the origin of our word "mile"?

(4) Make a brief statement about the first recorded sale of land.

(5) We often see the expression *casus belli* in our newspapers. Explain its meaning.

ANSWERS TO TEST QUESTIONS
No. 18.

Arithmetic.— (1) $124 : \times :: 93 : 162$.
$$\frac{124 \times 162}{93} = \frac{20088}{93} = 216 \text{ ft.} \quad Ans.$$

(2) Amount sent, $\$2,530 = 102.5$ per cent. of amount paid out.
$$\frac{2530}{102\,5} = \$2,468.29 +. \quad Ans.$$

(3) $1 \text{ gi} = \frac{1}{32} \text{ gal.} = .03125 \text{ gal.} \quad Ans.$

(4) 3600″ in 1°.

$$\therefore 1'' = \tfrac{1}{3600}°.$$

and $5'' = \tfrac{5}{3600}° = \tfrac{1}{720}°$. *Ans.*

(5) Longitude of San Francisco $= 122° 26' 15''$ W.
Longitude of Boston $= 71° 3' 30''$ W.
Difference in longitude $= 51° 22' 45''$.
Difference in time $= \tfrac{1}{15}$ of dif. in longitude.

$$\frac{51° 22' 45''}{15} = 3^{hrs} 25' 31''.$$

Since Boston is east of San Francisco, noon at Boston gives forenoon at San Francisco $= 3^{hrs}$ 25′ 31″ before noon $= 34'$ 29″ after 8 o'clock A. M. *Ans.*

Language and Grammar.— (1) Comparative, positive, superlative. Good, better, best; ill, worse, worst; little, less, least; much, more, most.

(2) A phrase having a peculiar sense not agreeing with the logical sense of its structural forms. I can make nothing of it. He is more than willing. I do observe you now, of late.

(3) (*a*) *Shall* we ever be satisfied? "Will" is never used interrogatively in the first person. (*b*) *Would* they be satisfied? In asking questions, the second and third person employ the auxiliary which is expected in reply. (*c*) *Should* we be satisfied, if we should go? "Would" and "should" are simply the past tenses of "shall" and "will," and follow the same rules. (*d*) You *should* be satisfied. Sometimes, as in this sentence, "should"

expresses duty or obligation. (*e*) Correct. See
(*c*) for reason.

(4) "Beware" has no past. *Might.* "Must"
has no past. *Should.* "Ought" has no past.

(5) (*a*) He did not pay more than $4 for the
hat. (*b*) An idiom that is rapidly growing in
favor, used for "superior ability." (*c*) A vulgar
expression for two. "Couple" has been used in
this sense by Carlyle, Addison, Dickens, Sir P.
Sidney, and others. (*d*) The authorities of the
university do the graduating or measuring, the
student is passive. Hence, "was graduated." (*e*)
Jeopard, instead of "jeopardize."

Geography. — (1) British Isles, United States,
British Isles.

(2) United States, France, Russia, Italy, Austro-
Hungary.

(3) Belgium, Egypt, Mauritius.

(4) China proper, Russia, India, British India,
United States.

(5) Brazil, Canadian Dominion, United States.

United States History. — (1) President Jackson
did not rely upon his first cabinet for advice; but
he counseled with a few of his favorites, some of
whom held subordinate positions in the depart-
ments. These men were called his "Kitchen
Cabinet," because of their inferior positions, and

because through them the President could be in-fluenced.

(2) In 1872, the "Modocs," a band of Indians living in southern Oregon, to avenge some of the tribe murdered by white men 20 years before, and to force the United States government to consent to a more favorable treaty in their behalf, began hostilities. After a bloody war they were completely conquered and removed to the Indian Territory. There, many of the survivors have become civilized, many Christians, and one or two ministers of the gospel.

(3) Savannah, presented to President Lincoln, on Christmas day, 1865.

(4) A Congress of 66 members, from 17 independent American states, which held sessions in Washington, D. C., during the latter months of 1889 and the opening months of 1890, and made many recommendations, the principal one being that international difficulties should be settled by arbitration and not by war.

(5) Robert C. Winthrop, of Massachusetts, composed the oration at the laying of the corner stone, and also that at the dedication of the Washington monument, 1848–1885. Daniel Webster, also of Massachusetts, performed the same services in connection with the Bunker Hill monument.

———

General Information.— (1) It means the levying of just enough tax on imports to meet the current expenses of the government.

(2) Roger Ascham.

(3) It is corrupted from the Latin word *mille*, a thousand. The Roman mile was a thousand paces. Hence, the name "mile" from *mille*.

(4) See Genesis, 23d chapter. Abraham bought a burial place for his family from Ephron, paying him 400 shekels of silver for it.

(5) *Casus belli* is a Latin phrase which means, in law and diplomacy, some act or circumstance which renders war inevitable or unavoidable.

PRONOUNCING CONTEST — No. 18.

Honor, onerous, immediate, indisputable, exemplary, papa, paw, pawpaw, cataclysm, catastrophe, iron, none, nun, financier, financially, finance, resume, *resume*, consomme, consume.

TEST QUESTIONS — No. 19.

Arithmetic.—(1) My watch gains 4⅔ minutes a day. If it is exactly correct at noon on July 4, what time will it show at 3 P. M. on September 4?

(2) A train travels 33¼ miles an hour. Making no allowance for stops, how far will it travel between 10½ minutes past 7 in the morning and 20½ minutes past 3 in the afternoon?

(3) A farmer wishing to ascertain the number of acres in a rectangular field, and having no measure, "steps" the distances. He finds the length to be 200 steps, the width 160 steps. His steps average 3¼ feet. How many acres are in the field?

(4) I have a gas jet which burns two feet of gas per hour. If I have it lighted 2½ hours every evening from October 1 to April 1, inclusive, how much will my gas bill amount to at $1.50 per 1,000 feet?

(5) I bought a stock of goods for $4,500. The freight was 7 per cent. of the cost. I sell 35 per cent. of the goods at a profit of 33⅓ per cent.; 45 per cent. at a profit of 25 per cent.; and the remainder at cost. What was my gain?

Language and Grammar.—(1) Give the plural of each of the following words, with your reasons: Negro, grotto, Cato.

(2) Give two abstract nouns which do not add s to form their plurals. Give two abstract nouns which do add s to form the plural.

(3) Name five nouns which have the plural form but are used in both numbers.

(4) Correct the following, and give reasons: " I am not certain whether I can come." " He is the same man as came yesterday."

(5) Give an illustration of a proverb; of an epithet; of elision.

Geography.—(1) Define the terms *low barometer* and *high barometer*.

(2) What are volcanic islands? coral islands? Name two of each.

(3) At the equator, at what elevation is the snow line reached?

(4) Starting from Manilla in a ship, and stopping on your way at Singapore, Cape Town, and Bahia, what islands and countries would you pass, and over what waters would you sail?

(5) Name the deepest fresh-water lake in America, and tell where it is situated.

United States History.—(1) What congress was in session 302 days?

(2) He was graduated at Princeton, was a lawyer, a United States senator, chancellor of a great university, president of a college, and was nomi-

nated for vice president of the United States. Name him.

(3) What are political assessments? When and where did they originate?

(4) Name all the places at which congress held its meetings between the beginning of the revolution and the removal to Washington?

(5) When were the most-noted commercial crises in United States history?

General Information.—(1) Give the origin of each of the following words: Agate, ague, disparage, fulsome, neighbor.

(2) Of two chapters in a certain book, one contains but 11 words, the other but 16. Name the book, and quote the contents of the two chapters.

(3) He was an eminent critic and essayist; he was imprisoned two years for attacking in a newspaper a royal personage; his father was at one time a lawyer in Philadelphia. Name him.

(4) Name the author of each of the following quotations:

"To know *thyself*—in others self concern;
  Wouldst thou know others? read thyself and learn."
"He that respects himself is safe from others;
  He wears a coat of mail that none can pierce."
"Silence more musical than any song."

(5) What was the origin of the interrogation and exclamation points?

ANSWERS TO TEST QUESTIONS

No. 19.

Arithmetic.— (1) Total number of days, $62\frac{1}{8}$. $4\frac{3}{4}$ minutes $\times 62\frac{1}{8} = 295$ minutes $= 4$ hours 55 minutes. Hence the watch at 3 P. M. on September 4 will show 7:55 P. M.

(2) The number of hours from $10\frac{1}{2}$ minutes past 7 A. M. until $20\frac{1}{2}$ minutes past 3 P. M. is 8 hours and 10 minutes. $33\frac{3}{4}$ minutes $\times 8\frac{1}{6} = 275\frac{5}{8}$ minutes.

(3) The length $= 650$ feet; width, 520 feet.
$$\frac{650 \times 520}{43560} = 7.7 + \text{acres.}$$

(4) From October 1 to April 1, inclusive $= 183$ evenings. Gas burned each evening, 5 feet. $5 \times 183 = 915$. $\$1.50 \times 915 = \$1.37$.

(5) $\$4,500 + 7\% = \$4,815.00$
     $4,815$ of $35\% = 1,685.25$
    $1,685 + 33\frac{1}{3}\% = 2,447.00$
     $4,815$ of $45\% = 2,166.75$
    $2,166.75 + 25\% = 2,708.44$
      Remainder $= 963.00$
$\$2,447 + 2,708.44 + 963 =$ total selling price $= \$6,118.44$. $\$6,118.44 - \$4,815 = \$1,303.44 =$ gain.

Language and Grammar.— (1) Negroes, grottos, Catos, Nouns ending in *o* preceded by a consonant generally form their plural by adding *es,*

Grotto is an exception to the rule. The plural of proper names ending in *o* is formed by adding *s*.

(2) (*a*) Meekness, decorum. (*b*) Affinities, gravities.

(3) News, alms, odds, gallows, bellows.

(4) (*a*) I am not certain whether I can come or not. The corresponding conjunction of *whether* is *or*, and the words *or not* should finish the sentence. (*b*) He is the same man *that* cames yesterday. *That* should be used after *same*.

(5) (*a*) A sentence which briefly and forcibly expresses some practical truth. Example: "All is not gold that glitters." (*b*) An adjective expressing some attribute, quality or relation that is properly or specially appropriate to a person or thing, as a *just* man; a *verdant* lawn.—*International Dictionary*. (*c*) The suppression of a vowel or syllable; usually in poetry. Examples: " 'T is he;" " I 'll ne'er forget."

Geography.— (1) The barometer is low when there is a great deal of vapor in the air, and the air is lighter than usual. A *low* barometer indicates a moist atmosphere. A *high* barometer indicates a heavy atmosphere, which may be due to denseness or dryness.

(2) They are formed by materials ejected by submarine volcanoes. Graham island, the Sandwich islands.

(3) Sixteen thousand feet.

(4) (*a*) From the Pacific ocean into the China sea, through the Strait of Malacca, on the Indian ocean, across the South Atlantic ocean. China, Anam, Borneo, Sumatra, Siam, Ceylon, Madagascar, Cape Colony.

(5) Crater lake, in Oregon. The average depth is 1,490 feet; deepest sounding, 1,196.

United States History.— (1) The thirty-first Congress.

(2) Theodore Frelinghuysen.

(3) (*a*) Contributions exacted of candidates for office and office-holders by state, congressional, national or municipal political committees, for the purpose of paying the expenses of campaigns. (*b*) The report of a committee to the twenty-fifth Congress states that a custom-house officer in New York was obliged to pay assessments. This is the first recorded case.

(4) Philadelphia, Baltimore, Lancaster, York, Princeton, Annapolis, Trenton, and New York.

(5) 1819, 1837, 1857, 1873, 1893.

General Information.— (1) (*a*) Named after the place in which it was first found, the river Achates, in Sicily. (*b*) From the French *aigue*, meaning sharp. (*c*) The French word *parage* means equality of birth; so, to place a man below his proper station is to *disparage* him. (*d*)

From the word *foulsome*. (*c*) From the two Anglo-Saxon words *boor* and *nigh*.

(2) In a translation of Horrebow's "The Natural History of Iceland," one chapter is headed "Concerning Owls." The chapter is as follows: "There are no owls of any kind in the whole island." Another chapter, in the same book, "Concerning Snakes," reads thus: "No snakes of any kind are to be met with throughout the whole of the island."

(3) Leigh Hunt.

(4) (*a*) Schiller. (*b*) Longfellow. (*c*) Christina G. Rossetti.

(5) The exclamation point originally was I placed above O, thus, $\frac{I}{O}$. The interrogation point was formed by placing Q above O, thus, $\frac{Q}{O}$.

PRONOUNCING CONTEST — No. 19.

Clinique, Elizabethan, grimaces, calf, absolutory, antimony, antinomy, requiem, panegyrized, Tehuantepec, raspberries, incognito, anachronisms, soothe, breathe, turquois, pantheon, parthenon, Millais, millet.

www.ingramcontent.com/pod-product-compliance
Lightning Source LLC
Chambersburg PA
CBHW020549270326

41927CB00006B/772